WORLD BIBLIOGRAPHICAL SERIES
General Editors:
Robert L. Collison (Editor-in-chief)
Sheila R. Herstein
Louis J. Reith
Hans H. Wellisch

VOLUME 13

France

THE WORLD BIBLIOGRAPHICAL SERIES

This series will eventually cover every country in the world, each in a separate volume comprising annotated entries on works dealing with its history, geography, economy and politics; and with its people, their culture, customs, religion and social organization. Attention will also be paid to current living conditions – housing, education, newspapers, clothing etc. – that are all too often ignored in standard bibliographies; and to those particular aspects relevant to individual countries. Each volume seeks to achieve, by use of careful selectivity and critical assessment of the literature, an expression of the country and an appreciation of its nature and national aspirations, to guide the reader towards an understanding of its importance. The keynote of the series is to provide, in a uniform format, an interpretation of each country that will express its culture, its place in the world, and the qualities and background that make it unique.

OTHER VOLUMES IN THE SERIES
1 *Yugoslavia*, John J. Horton
2 *Lebanon*, Shereen Khairallah
3 *Lesotho*, Shelagh M. Willet and David Ambrose
4 *Rhodesia/Zimbabwe*, Oliver B. Pollak and Karen Pollak
5 *Saudi Arabia*, Frank A. Clements
6 *USSR*, Anthony Thompson
7 *South Africa*, Reuben Musiker
8 *Malawi*, Robert B. Boeder
9 *Guatemala*, Woodman B. Franklin
10 *Pakistan*, S. Aleem Qureishi
11 *Uganda*, Robert L. Collison
12 *Malaysia*, Lim Huck Tee
14 *Panama*, Eleanor Langstaff
15 *Hungary*, Thomas Kabdebo
16 *USA*, Sheila R. Herstein and Naomi Robbins
17 *Greece*, Richard Clogg and Mary Jo Clogg
18 *New Zealand*, R. F. Grover
19 *Algeria*, Richard Lawless

Frances Chambers
*Assistant Professor,
Library Department,
City College of New York*

France
Edited by Sheila R. Herstein

CLIO PRESS
OXFORD, ENGLAND · SANTA BARBARA, CALIFORNIA

Copyright © 1980 by Clio Press Ltd.

All rights reserved. No part of this publication may be reproduced, stored in any retrieval system, or transmitted in any form or by any means, electronic, mechanical, photocopying or otherwise, without the prior permission in writing of the publishers.

British Library Cataloguing in Publication Data

Chambers, Frances
    France.–(World bibliographical series; 13).
    1. France – Bibliography
    I. Title   II. Series
    016.944   Z2161

ISBN 0-903450-25-9

Designed by Bernard Crossland
Computer typeset by Peter Peregrinus Ltd.
Printed in Great Britain
by T. & A. Constable Ltd., Edinburgh

Clio Press Ltd.,
Woodside House, Hinksey Hill,
Oxford OX1 5BE, England.
Providing the services of the European
Bibliographical Centre and the American
Bibliographical Center.

American Bibliographical Center-Clio Press,
Riviera Campus, 2040 Alameda Padre Serra,
Santa Barbara, Ca. 93103, U.S.A.

Contents

INTRODUCTION ix

THE COUNTRY AND ITS PEOPLE 1

GEOGRAPHY 6
    General   6   Travel guides   9
    Maps   8

ARCHAEOLOGY AND PREHISTORY 11

HISTORY 13
    General   13   Modern France—General,
    Roman Gaul   15   1715 to the present   21
    Middle Ages   15   Eighteenth century   22
    Renaissance   18   Nineteenth century   27
    Seventeenth century   19   Twentieth century   30

FOLKLORE 38

RELIGION 40

PHILOSOPHY AND INTELLECTUAL LIFE 43
    General   43   Nineteenth century   46
    Eighteenth century   44   Twentieth century   46

SOCIAL AND POLITICAL THEORY 49

SOCIAL CLASS, SOCIAL GROUPS, AND
SOCIAL CHANGE 53

EDUCATION 58

v

Contents

NATIONALITIES AND MINORITIES....................62

STATISTICS...66

POLITICS...68

POLITICAL PARTIES, GROUPS AND MOVEMENTS......71

FOREIGN RELATIONS..................................75

GOVERNMENT AND ADMINISTRATION...............80

LAW AND CONSTITUTION..........................86

ECONOMICS...88

FINANCE AND BANKING.............................93

BUSINESS AND INDUSTRY...........................94

FASHION...96

TRADE UNIONS AND LABOUR MOVEMENTS...........97

AGRICULTURE..100

TRANSPORT...102

ENVIRONMENT......................................103

FOOD AND DRINK..................................105

SCIENCE AND TECHNOLOGY........................107

LANGUAGE...110
    General   110   Dictionaries   111

LITERATURE..112
    General   112   Contemporary   116
    History and criticism   113

Contents

ART 119

ARCHITECTURE AND CITY PLANNING 122

MUSIC AND DANCE 125

THEATRE AND FILM 128

PUBLISHING AND THE PRESS 130

NEWSPAPERS, MAGAZINES AND PERIODICALS 132
    Dailies   132   Weeklies, monthlies, etc.   134

PERIODICALS PUBLISHED OUTSIDE FRANCE 137

ENCYCLOPAEDIAS AND DIRECTORIES 138

MUSEUMS, ARCHIVES AND LIBRARIES 140

BIBLIOGRAPHIES 143

INDEX OF AUTHORS, TITLES AND SUBJECTS 145

MAP OF FRANCE 177

Introduction

This bibliography applies an area studies approach to France: it is a compilation of references to books and articles that deal with all aspects of French life and culture.

It goes without saying that a bibliography of 542 books and articles is not comprehensive: I have thought of this book as a 'core' collection of books about France for an English-speaking reader who has a serious interest in the country and its culture, but who is not a specialist. For such a reader, I have tried to select books that are starting points in various subject fields, or that are classic works, or indispensable reading, or thorough summaries. I have also tried to cover as many aspects of France as possible, in order to serve the reader who wants to know about the Alsatians, as well as the one who wants to read about French politics. And I have tried to include books which themselves offer bibliographical guidance.

The main omissions in this work are of books on single individuals, standard works in French, and bibliographic and research tools. The number of outstanding Frenchmen and Frenchwomen who have had books written about them made the first omission necessary. For the standard French works in the subject fields covered in this book, I refer the reader to John E. Pemberton's *How to find out about France* (q.v.). Those whose need is for bibliographic and research tools will find up-to-date information on these in *An annotated bibliography of French language and literature* (q.v.) by Fernande Bassan and others.

The annotations are meant to be informative and to encourage a browsing approach. As this work is the result of sifting a mountain of printed material, I am certain that errors have crept in, and for these the reader has my apology. If the reader is encouraged to consult the books listed here, I will feel that my work is successful.

My gratitude goes to everyone who has helped me in compiling this book. In particular I wish to thank Carole Banko, Esq., of the library of John Jay College of Criminal Justice, New York City,

Introduction

and Arthur Knieriem and Sheila Herstein of the library of the City College of New York. I also wish to thank the librarians of New York University and of Yale University for their courtesy in allowing me to review in their libraries many of the books listed in this bibliography.

New York City, 1979

The Country and its People

1 **The civilization of France.**
E. R. Curtius, translated from the German by O. Wyon. New York: Macmillan, 1932. 247p. Reprinted, Plainview, New York: Books for Libraries. (Select Bibliographies Reprint series).
Although written nearly fifty years ago, this remains a classic work on the French cultural outlook. In an analysis informed by a brilliant intelligence, the author guides the reader to an understanding of French civilization by tracing values and ideologies to their natural and historical bases. France has changed in many ways since Curtius wrote, but this book could still be profitably read today by those probing the French point of view in any field.

2 **France, steadfast and changing.**
Raymond Aron, translated from the French by J. Irwin, L. Einaudi. Cambridge, Massachusetts: Harvard University Press, 1960. 201p.
In 1957 the author delivered three lectures at Harvard University analysing the French political régime, France's economic development, and the French Union. They are collected in this volume, along with a postscript on the first year of the De Gaulle government. From his consideration of the political, economic, and colonial aspects of his country, Aron concludes that France is 'unpredictable in her sudden reversals, constant in her fundamental impulses'.

3 **France.**
Patrick E. Charvet. New York: Praeger, 1955. 254p. map. bibliog.
A perceptive and well-presented, although now somewhat dated, venture into the analysis of the French, whom the author sums up as 'individualists, idealists, realists, universalists, authoritarians, paternalists, and formalists'. The emphasis is

1

The Country and its People

placed on the political scene, with Charvet seeking to bring to light the assumptions and permanent features which underlie French politics.

4 The spirit of France.
Paul Cohen-Portheim, translated from the French by Alan Harris. New York: Dutton, 1933. 215p.

An older book, with a somewhat mystical approach to national character. The author identifies the 'French genius' as the 'purely European genius' and sets himself the task in this book of tracing the historical development of the traditions of French culture.

5 The French, portrait of a people.
Sanche de Gramont. New York: Putnam, 1969. 479p.

An attempt 'to isolate Frenchness', this book is itself a good example of Gallic wit. The author gives a lively, anecdotal account of contemporary French culture, exploring the contradictions of *mystique*, *esprit*, and *savoir-vivre*. Outspoken chapters discuss language, Paris, women, art, pleasure, politics, and sex. Strangely enough, since this book was published its author has changed his name to Ted Morgan and emigrated to the United States.

6 The culture of France in our time.
Julian Park. Ithaca, New York: Cornell University Press, 1954. 345p. bibliog.

The 'our time' of the title refers to the 1930s, 1940s, and 1950s, and the volume is a collection of essays discussing literature, art, theatre, music, philosophy, education, religion, law, and science in France during these years. Most of the contributors are Americans.

7 As France goes.
David Schoenbrunn. New York: Harper, 1957. 341p.

A fast-paced journalistic account of the Fourth Republic. Although now outdated, the book provides abundant facts and some interesting insights into French character.

8 France: a study in nationality.
Andre Siegfried. New Haven, Connecticut: Yale University Press, 1930. 122p.

The author was a French conservative who in this short book undertook the task of analysing French psychology and identifying the conditions under which French character is formed. According to him, 'negative individualism' is the key to French attitudes: a Frenchman is an individualist who desires to be self-sufficient. He also concludes that the essence of the French nation lies in a social, not a political, consensus.

The Country and its People

9 **Mythologies.**
Roland Barthes, selected and translated from the French by Annette Lavers. New York: Hill & Wang; London: Cape, 1972. 158p.

A semiological analysis of French society, 1954-56. In this collection of short essays, the author captures, dissects, and demystifies such everyday French cultural phenomena as wrestling, striptease, steak and chips, and Einstein's brain, deciphering the meaning of these supposedly realistic objects and acts and exposing the part that they play in reinforcing the ideology of the French ruling class. A provocative book.

10 **The New France.**
John Ardagh. Harmondsworth, England: Penguin Books, 1977. 3rd ed. 733p. maps. bibliog. (Pelican Books).

Since the end of the Second World War, the French have revitalized their economy, industries, agriculture, and trade. They have tried to upgrade the provinces and to renovate Paris. These have been years of suburbanization, women's liberation, and student unrest, with Catholicism becoming dynamic and communism conservative, and the cinema outstripping the other arts. This book is highly recommended to those wishing to understand the changes that have produced the 'New France'.

11 **Englishmen, Frenchmen, Spaniards.**
Salvador de Madariaga. London: Oxford University Press, 1929. 251p. Reprinted, New York: Hill and Wang, 1969.

This venture into comparative ethnopsychology by a distinguished Spanish writer and diplomat reappeared in print briefly in 1969. Readers who can locate either printing will find its tri-ethnic perspective stimulating. Another vintage analysis of the French character by a foreigner, out of print but still worth reading, is Friedrich Sieberg's *Who are these French?* (New York, 1932).

12 **France against herself: a perceptive study of France's past, her politics, and her unending crises.**
Herbert Luethy, translated from the German by Eric Mosbacher. New York: Praeger, 1955. 476p. (Books That Matter).

Although written in 1953, this book continues to be cited as one of the best discussions of the French character as it evinces itself in politics. The author centres his analysis on the force that history exerts in France - a force with which contemporary Frenchmen must contend in their political struggles.

13 **The rules of the game in Paris.**
Nathan C. Leites, translated from the French by Derek Coltman. Chicago, Illinois: University of Chicago Press, 1969. 355p.

Under such headings as 'The rut and the sense of adventure' and 'Velvet glove and iron hand', the author presents passages, for the most part extracted from printed sources, that contrast the paradoxes of French character. He freely admits 'the inadequacy of [his] data and their motley character', but feels that they

3

The Country and its People

serve his purpose in the book: 'to achieve an evocation of the nuances in a certain climate'. A book that is fun for Francophiles.

14 **The new France.**
Edward R. Tannenbaum. Chicago, Illinois: University of Chicago Press, 1961. 251p. bibliog.

This study of France circa 1960 is organized around the theme of cultural forces in conflict. His 'Notes on sources' at the end of the volume is an excellent bibliography of books and articles on French culture.

15 **In search of France.**
Stanley Hoffmann, Charles P. Kindleberger, Laurence Wylie, Jesse R. Pitts, Jean-Baptiste Duroselle, Francois Goguel. Cambridge, Massachusetts: Harvard University Press, 1963. 443p. bibliog.

Prepared under the auspices of the Center for International Affairs, Harvard University, this book is perhaps the best of the several symposium volumes on the 'New France'. The six essays by distinguished scholars both summarize and elucidate the postwar era. Essays and their authors: 'Paradoxes of the French political community' (Hoffman); 'The postwar resurgence of the French economy' (Kindleberger); 'Social change at the grass roots' (Wylie); 'Continuity and change in bourgeois France' (Pitts); 'Changes in French foreign policy since 1945' (Duroselle); 'Six authors in search of a national character' (Goguel).

16 **Themes in French culture.**
Rhoda Metraux, Margaret Mead (and others). Stanford, California: Stanford University Press, 1954. 120p. bibliog. (Hoover Institute Studies, Series D: Communities, no. 1).

In this book the French are studied 'within an anthropological framework' by several anthropologists and writers, foremost among them being Margaret Mead. The study is 'focused on primary group relations, particularly in the *foyer*', and seeks to define 'the sense of community - the tie that binds - among Frenchmen'. The first section of the book is most interesting, covering the education of the child in the home and attempting a picture of how the outside world appears to the child. The second part of the volume consists of three background papers: 'The family in the French civil code', 'An analysis of fantasy in French film', and 'An analysis of French projective tests'.

17 **Conflict in France: the decline and fall of a stereotype.**
John Frears. *Political Studies*, vol. 20, pt. 1 (March 1972), p. 31-41.

A refreshing article that takes Anglo-Saxon political scientists to task for their obsession with 'the academic stereotype of an unstable, divided, unruly French national character'. Frears proposes that the Anglo-Saxon world 'drop the whole notion of France as a model of a conflict society, even though it sustains Anglo-American myths'. He believes that while 'the tradition of conflict remains alive in France', there is now a real political consensus in the nation, 'based on the common patterns of an increasingly industrialized society'.

The Country and its People

18 **The French: how they live and work.**
Joseph T. Carroll. New York: Praeger, 1978. New rev. ed. 180p. (How They Live and Work, no. 7).

At present, this is the most up-to-date of the several available handbooks that present the basic facts on the structure of contemporary French life. Succinct chapters cover the country's geography, language, government and administration, housing, industries, education, amusements, transportation, and communications.

19 **France in the twentieth century.**
Philip Ouston. London: Macmillan, 1972. 290p. maps. bibliog.

An introduction to contemporary France. The first part of the book describes the nation's geography, social classes, economy, and politics; the second part covers the structure of the French government and administration; the third section surveys the social, cultural, and political history of France since the establishment of the Third Republic.

Geography

General

20 **France, a geographical survey.**
Philippe Pinchemel, translated from the French by Christine Trollope, Arthur J. Hunt. New York: Praeger, 1969. 454p. maps. bibliog.
A work that covers all aspects of geography except the purely economic, this is an excellent presentation of the natural features of France, its population, political structures, resources, agriculture, industry, and cities. The text is followed by a critical bibliography that summarizes the literature of French geography, listing both classic and recent work in French, as well as recommended atlases and maps. This translation has been prepared from the second French edition, incorporating the author's revisions for the third French edition.

21 **France: a geographical study.**
Pierre George, translated from the French by I. B. Thompson. New York: Barnes & Noble, 1974. 228p. maps. bibliog.
The author, a well-known French geographer, follows a traditional approach in this book. His work is authoritative and, as one reviewer comments, 'can take its place among classic descriptions of France'.

22 **France.**
Jacqueline Beaujeu-Garnier, with a foreword by J. M. Houston. London, New York: Longmans, 1975. 132p. bibliog. (The World's Landscapes).
This brief, competent volume by a well-known French geographer traces the patterns of man's interaction with his physical environment in France.

Geography. General

23 **France: its geography and growth.**
Jean Dollfuss, translated from the French by J.
Paterson. London: John Murray, 1972. 127p. maps.

A book written for the general reader. The text is enhanced by many striking photographs.

24 **Modern France: a social and economic geography.**
Ian B. Thompson. London: Butterworth, 1970. 465p. maps. bibliog.

Written to provide the English-speaking student with access to material analysing 'the structural and spatial changes which have transformed France since World War II'. The first part of the book, 'Patterns of social development', deals with manpower and population; the second part, 'Patterns of economic activity', discusses planned (and unplanned) growth and the infrastructure of the economy. A third part consists of essays analysing problems of social and economic development in each of France's twenty-two planning districts.

25 **Problem Regions of Europe series.**
Edited by D. I. Scargill. London, New York: Oxford University Press, 1973-76.

It is surprising to think of the European continent as underdeveloped, but it is around this concept that the Oxford University Press series Problem Regions of Europe has been organized. Five French regions have been included for analysis because of problems of agricultural enervation, urban sprawl, or hostile physical environment: *The Massif Central* (by H. D. Clout, 1973); *The Paris Basin* (by I. B. Thompson, 1973); *The Franco-Belgian border region* (by H. D. Clout, 1975); *The Saar-Lorraine* (by D. Burtenshaw, 1976); and *The Lower Rhone and Marseille* (by I. B. Thompson, 1976).

26 **France from the air.**
Raymond Chevallier, Francois Cali, translated from the French by R. Greaves. New York: Norton, 1972. 318p.

A book of 193 aerial photographs, including 27 in colour. The emphasis is on historic, traditional France - chateaux, monasteries, cathedrals, landscape. Little attention is given to modern, industrial France. A splendid but one-sided view of France in the 1970s.

27 **Climates of Northern and Western Europe.**
Edited by C. C. Wallen. Amsterdam, London, New York: Elsevier, 1970, p. 135-93. (World Survey of Climatology, vol. 5).

Chapter 4 of this work, 'The climate of France, Belgium, the Netherlands and Luxembourg', is a convenient summary of such meteorological information as the nonspecialist English reader might wish to have about France. Begins with a brief overview of the historical development of the collection of weather data in France - a field of endeavour that has a long history there - and then gives technical meteorological data on climatic factors, seasonal variations, air circulation, and temperature. Includes more than thirty-five climatic tables for the regions of the country. The references appended to the chapter refer the reader to the standard French sources in the field.

Geography. Maps

28 **Quality of life in France.**
P. L. Knox, A. Scarth. *Geography*, vol. 62, pt. 1 (Jan. 1977), p. 9-16.

A brief but valuable article that analyses the regional social geography of France and concludes that the 'quality of life' in France has a 'strong regional component which does not correspond to any of the subdivisions conventionally recognized by geographers'. The authors use forty-one variables - some objective, some subjective - to rank the departments according to their capacity for providing *la douceur de vivre*.

29 **A considerable town.**
M. F. K. Fisher. New York: Knopf, 1978. 208p.

At last! A book that abandons tired stereotypes to take a fresh look at Marseille. The author, best known for her gastronomical writings, has produced an entertaining and informative volume that reveals the humanity and dignity of the Mediterranean port and its inhabitants.

30 **Granite island: a portrait of Corsica.**
Dorothy Carrington. London: Longman, 1971. 336p. bibliog.

An account of Corsica based on both personal contact and research. The author provides much historical, archaeological, and anthropological information to illuminate contemporary Corsica.

31 **Discovering the Camargue.**
Monica Krippner. London: Hutchinson, 1960. 207p.

A personal but well-informed account of one of the most singular regions of France, the Île de la Camargue, an area of marshes and plains where the traveller finds 'cowboys', rice fields, and the French version of the bullfight. All aspects of the Camargue and its inhabitants are described in this book. The Camargue, like all of France, is changing: the author closes her book with a chapter on the approaching transformations and the uncertain future of a unique way of life.

Maps

32 **Carte de France.** (Map of France.)
Paris: Institut Geographique, 1878-, continuously revised. Scale: 1:20,000.

The *Carte de France*, produced and maintained by the Institut Geographique National, is the official map of France; the sheets of its 1:20,000 series are the basis for cartographic work for the country.

33 **Nouvelle carte de France.** (New map of France.)
Paris: Institut Geographique National, 1967. Scale 1:100,000.

A map of France on an intermediate scale in 292 sheets.

Geography. Travel guides

34 **Cartes Michelins.** (Michelin maps.)
Paris: Michelin. Scale: 1:200,000.
Carefully prepared, well-presented dependable road maps for all regions of France.

35 **Atlas de France.** (Atlas of France.)
Comité National Français de Geographie. Paris: Editions Geographiques de France, 1951-59. 2nd ed. 2 vols. maps.
The French can be justifiably proud of their national atlas, a superior example of cartographic expertise. Its maps cover physical geography, geomorphology, climatology, biogeography, hydrography, economic geography, and human and political geography.

36 **Atlas historique de la France contemporaine, 1800-1965.** (Historical atlas of contemporary France, 1800-1965.)
P. A. Bouju. Paris: Armand Colin, 1966. 234p. maps.
Demographic, economic, political, religious, educational, cultural, and colonial aspects of France during 165 years are cartographically presented on this volume's 461 maps.

37 **Atlas historique et culturel de la France.** (Historical and cultural atlas of France.)
Jacques Broussard. Paris: Elsevier, 1957. 214p. maps. bibliog.
This reference source contains maps and illustrations tracing cultural and historical developments in France from prehistoric times to the Fourth Republic. A very useful tool for the student of history, literature, architecture, or art.

Travel guides

38 **Michelin Red Guide: France.**
Paris: Michelin, Services de Tourisme, 1979.
The latest edition of the Michelin Red Guide is the indispensable handbook for those who wish to sample the best in France. Its graded selections of hotels and restaurants are exhaustively researched for each annual revision. The text is available in English, French, German, and Italian. A *Michelin Red Guide to Paris* is also published.

39 **Michelin Green Guide series.**
Paris: Michelin, Services de Tourisme.
The books in the Michelin Green Guide series cover the regions of France in less detail than the Red Guides, but remain good choices for those who wish for reliable guidance in touring France. Currently available: *The Chateaux of the Loire*, *The French Riviera*, *Normandy*, *Paris*, and *Brittany*. Books in the Green Guide series are not revised annually.

Geography. Travel guides

40 **Fodor's France.**
New York: David McKay, 1979. 550p.
An often-revised guidebook, part of a travel series aimed at the budget-minded. Illustrated with colour and black-and-white photographs. Includes city plans and an English-French tourist vocabulary.

41 **The Blue Guide to Paris.**
Edited by Stuart Rossiter. London: Benn; New York: Rand McNally, 1968. 236p. maps. bibliog.
A detailed guide to Paris for those with an interest in history, art and architecture. The first part of the book describes nineteen touring routes; the second section covers the Louvre and twelve other Parisian collections, including the Bibliothèque Nationale; and the final section gives information on five excursions from Paris: Versailles, Vincennes, Malmaison, Saint-Denis and Chantilly, and Fontainebleau. A short bibliography lists English books that can introduce the traveller to Paris.

Archaeology and Prehistory

42 **Brittany.**
P. R. Giot, in collaboration with J. L'Helgouach, J. Briard. London: Thames & Hudson; New York: Praeger, 1960. 272p. bibliog. (Ancient People and Places, vol. 13).
A book intended to be 'a conspectus of archaeological information on Brittany, which will not only be of value to archaeologists and students, but will also awaken the interest of laymen' in ancient Armorica. The text discusses the remains of the prehistoric and protohistoric cultures that succeeded each other in the region, with a chapter devoted to those enigmatic monuments, the menhirs.

43 **Celts and Gallo-Romans.**
Jean-Jacques Hatt, translated from the French by James Hogarth. Geneva: Nagel, 1970. 333p. maps. bibliog. (Archaeologia Mundi).
A book that contains both an admirable synthesis of what is known of the Celts and Gallo-Romans who lived in the territory now called France, and an informed presentation of the interests, methods, and techniques of present-day French archaeology. The first chapter traces the history of archaeological research in France since the 17th century; the second and third chapters discuss current methods and techniques and the themes around which 20th century French archaeology centres. The final chapters give the results of archaeological research, and include a discussion of the La Tène culture, the Romans in Gaul, and various aspects of Gallo-Roman civilization.

Archaeology and Prehistory

44 **France before the Romans.**
Stuart Piggott, Glynn Daniels, Charles McBurney (and others). London: Thames & Hudson, 1975. 233p. maps. bibliog.

An excellent book that summarizes for students and scholars much of what is known about France from the beginnings up to the Roman Conquest and the establishment of Roman Gaul. Each section of the book has been contributed by an expert who discusses a separate aspect of pre-Roman Gaul in up-to-date detail.

History

General

45 France: an interpretive history.
Ernest John Knapton. New York: Scribner's, 1971. 616p. bibliog.

Knapton presents the history of France 'as a segment of the larger history of Europe and indeed of the world', including cultural and social events as well as political and diplomatic. His presentation is readable, with the emphasis on factual recounting rather than interpretation (in spite of his subtitle). This is a solid work, a good starting place for the general reader to get an overview of the French historical experience. The bibliography is extensive.

46 A history of France.
André Maurois, translated by Henry L. Binsse, Gerard Hopkins. New York: Farrar, Straus, & Cudahy, 1957. 598p. maps.

Maurois is best known as the author of lengthy, popular biographies of such romantic literary figures as Balzac, George Sand, and Lord Byron. When he turns to the history of his own country, one expects that the story will be told with a great deal of literary style. The general reader will find this volume enjoyable reading. Although the book is no longer in print, most public libraries probably own a copy.

47 A short history of France from early times to 1972.
Herbert Butterfield (and others). London: Cambridge University Press, 1974. 2nd ed. with new material. 246p. maps.

A reliable account of the history of France, originally prepared by British Naval Intelligence for a four-volume *Handbook on France* and admirably condensed for this edition. Sections are contributed by distinguished British historians, J. Hampden Jackson, H. C. Darby, D. W. Brogan, N. J. M. Richardson, and the editor. The second edition has a postscript covering events up to the elections of 1973.

History. General

48 A history of French civilization.
Georges Duby, Robert Mandrou, translated from the French by James Blakely Atkinson. New York: Random House, 1964. 626p. bibliog.

This excellent short history of France, from the year 1000 to 1956, by two distinguished French historians, provides a well-rounded view of French civilization. Emphasis is on the milieu of each period: the authors note intellectual, economic, social, and psychological factors at work and relate them to political events. The work is a superior presentation of the movement of ideas in France. The bibliography lists French sources.

49 France: a modern history.
Albert L. Guerard. Ann Arbor, Michigan: University of Michigan Press, 1969. New ed., revised and enlarged by Paul Gagnon. 578p. maps. bibliog. (University of Michigan History of the Modern World).

According to Guerard, France was born at Strasbourg in 842, when Charles the Bold and Louis the German pledged their aid to each other against Lothair. Guerard states his purpose to be the writing of the 'biography' of the nation, 'how France grew, in territory, in organization, but above all in consciousness'. Whether or not in sympathy with this anthropomorphic approach, the reader will find the book a reliable, vigorously presented survey. The bibliography is comprehensive. Unfortunately, it was not brought up to date for the revised edition: except for the section on the Fifth Republic, work done after 1959 is not listed. Guerard is also the author of a straightforward brief account of French history, *France: a short history* (New York: Norton, 1946), which remains in print thirty years after its first appearance.

50 Modern France: a companion to French studies.
Edited by A. Tilley. Cambridge, England: Cambridge University Press, 1922. 850p. bibliog. Reprinted: New York: Russell, 1967.

A mini-encyclopaedia of 400 years of French history and culture, 1500 to 1914. Although over fifty years old, this book contains much detailed information that is still useful, and librarians will be pleased to know that it is still in print. Separate sections, each prepared by an expert, cover the army, the navy, economic and social life, the law, education and learning, literature, architecture, painting, sculpture and the decorative arts, music, theatre, philosophy, and science. A bibliography of French sources follows each section.

51 Fleur de lys: the kings and queens of France.
Joy Law. New York: McGraw-Hill; London: Hamish Hamilton, 1976. 256p. bibliog.

A history of the rulers of France from Hugh Capet to Charles X, focusing on the personal rather than the political. Contemporary accounts of the royal personages, from letters, memoirs, and journals, are incorporated into the text and lend immediacy to the narrative. The book is pleasantly illustrated. Genealogical tables clarify questions of descent and relationship.

Roman Gaul

52 **Roman France.**
Paul MacKendrick. New York: St. Martin's Press, 1972.
275p. maps. bibliog.
A cultural history, based on archaeological evidence. The contents of the volume are not circumscribed by the title: the book begins with the palaeolithic era of the Lascaux cave painting, and reaches into the present with a final chapter surveying Roman-inspired architecture in contemporary France. The main body of the book, however, does concentrate on Gaul as a Roman colony, 58 B.C. to 511 A.D.: sections on the war between the Romans and the Celts, Gaul under the Roman Empire, and the architecture, arts, crafts, and religion of the Gallo-Romans.

53 **Roman Gaul.**
Olwen Brogan. Cambridge, Massachusetts: Harvard University Press, 1953. 250p. maps. bibliog.
This is a very well-executed survey, designed 'to serve as an introduction to students and travellers who may wish to get a general picture of Roman Gaul'. It is based on scholarly sources and manages to be both informative and entertaining. Topics covered: Gaul and the Republic of Rome; Gaul and the Roman Empire; the towns and the countryside; Gallo-Roman industries and commerce, art and religion. Provides many details that illuminate social and cultural relations between Rome and Gaul. Illustrated with both drawings and photographs.

Middle Ages

54 **The history of the Franks.**
Gregory of Tours, translated from the Latin by Lewis Thorpe. Harmondsworth, England; Baltimore, Maryland: Penguin Books, 1974. 710p. bibliog. (Penguin Classics).
Gregory was Bishop of Tours from 573 until his death in 594. He was a Gallo-Roman, whose native tongue was 6th century Latin, and he wrote his *Historia Francorum* in that language. Present-day readers will find his eyewitness account of the era of the Merovingian kings vivid and dramatic. The Penguin edition has an extremely helpful introduction on Gregory and his times. A 20th century assessment of *The history of the Franks*, 'The work of Gregory of Tours in the light of modern research', is included in Wallace-Hadrill's collection, *The long-haired kings and other studies in Frankish history* (see next item).

55 **The long-haired kings and other studies in Frankish history.**
J. M. Wallace-Hadrill. New York: Barnes & Noble; London: Methuen, 1962. 261p.
A collection of essays on Frankish history; the longest study, which gives its title to the volume, is 'a study of a particular kind of barbarian kingship...not a political history of the Merovingian kings'. The other essays are 'Frankish Gaul', 'Gothia and Romania', 'The work of Gregory of Tours in the light of modern

History. Middle Ages

research', 'Fredegar and the history of France', and 'Archbishop Hincmar and the authorship of Lex Salica'.

56 Early medieval history.
J. M. Wallace-Hadrill. Oxford, England: Blackwell, 1975. 247p. bibliog.

A collection that focuses on British mediaeval history, but contains two essays of interest to students of early mediaeval France: 'The *Via Regia* of the Carolingian age' discusses political theory, and 'The Vikings in France' is an accessible study of the invasion of France by the men from the North.

57 Feudal society.
Marc Bloch, translated from the French by L. A. Manyon. Chicago, Illinois: University of Chicago Press; London, Routledge & Kegan Paul, 1961. 498p. bibliog.

Despite later work, Bloch's study of the society of the Middle Ages should be read by everyone seeking to understand the period. Bloch's aim in his book was to grasp the spirit in which the feudal age understood its institutions. In order to achieve this purpose, he drew his data from a wide area, taking into consideration much more than the formal patterns of authority: he studied the environment, the conditions under which ordinary life was led, and the mental climate that validated feudalism as a type of social and political organization.

58 Slavery and serfdom in the Middle Ages: selected essays.
Marc Bloch, translated from the French by William R. Beer. Berkeley, California: University of California Press, 1975. 276p. (Publications of the Center for Medieval and Renaissance Studies, UCLA, 8).

These six essays, selected and translated from Bloch's *Mélanges historiques*, concentrate on a particular aspect of feudal society and are important for the study of the class structure of the Middle Ages. Topics covered include the end of ancient slavery, ideas of personal liberty and servitude, the formation of the servile class, and the institution of serfdom.

59 Daily life in the world of Charlemagne.
Pierre Riché, translated from the French with an introduction by Jo Ann McNamara. Philadelphia, Pennsylvania: University of Pennsylvania Press, 1978. 380p. bibliog.

The author, professor of the history of the Middle Ages at the University of Paris X, has used primary sources to depict the Carolingian Empire of the 8th and 9th centuries from the perspective of its own times. Thus, rather than seeing this world as the first step in the development of Europe and the forerunner of a brilliant indigenous civilization, the reader receives a truer picture of a society of struggle and violence.

History. Middle Ages

60 The age of Charlemagne.
Donald A. Bullough. New York: Putnam; London: Elek, 1973. 2nd ed. 212p. maps. bibliog. (The Making of History).

At first glance, this is a book that might be mistaken for a coffee-table item because of its splendid illustrations. A closer perusal, however, proves it to be a very competent presentation of the history and culture of the Carolingian Empire. The illustrations are well-integrated into the narrative and show objects of historical as well as artistic interest. Good sections on Carolingian art, architecture, and education.

61 Chivalry.
Léon Gautier, translated from the French by D. C. Dunning, edited by Jacques Levran. London: Phoenix House; New York: Barnes & Noble, 1965. 345p.

An older book, written in the 1880s by a zealous champion of the Middle Ages. Gautier was a scholar and palaeographer who gathered together in this book the customs and usages pertaining to mediaeval knighthood. As he drew much of his material from the *chansons de geste*, the knight appears in his ideal form. The reader must make allowances for this idealization and for a 19th century point of view, but the book is useful for an understanding of the manners of France in the Middle Ages.

62 Later medieval France: the polity.
Peter Lewis. London: Macmillan; New York: St. Martin's Press, 1968. 418p. maps.

The author writes for the historian rather than the general reader, but no library collection would wish to be without his book, which has been called the 'most important contribution to the understanding of French society on the eve of modern times'. The question of power in 15th century France is thoroughly explored in all its manifestations in the social and political life of the times: the church, the king, the structure of government, representative institutions, and social classes.

63 The Norman Empire.
John Le Patourel. Oxford, England: Clarendon Press; New York: Oxford University Press, 1976. 416p. maps. bibliog.

An up-to-date work on the Normans that focuses on the political structure and organization of their 'empire' in Northern France and Britain. Traces the history of the expansion of the Normans from the early 10th century to the 12th, placing the Normans' conquest of England in the context of their European activities.

64 French chivalry: chivalric ideas and practices in mediaeval France.
Sidney Painter. Baltimore, Maryland: Johns Hopkins Press, 1940. Reprinted, 1966. 179p.

A graceful presentation of the ideas that underlay the mediaeval institution of chivalry. Painter discusses feudal chivalry, religious chivalry, and courtly love, giving an account of their ideals and practices - and of the clashes between them, for, as he points out, 'the three types of chivalry were to some extent irreconci-

History. Renaissance

lable'. The book also includes a chapter on the noble class in France during the Middle Ages.

65 **The chivalrous society.**
Georges Duby, translated from the French by Cynthia Postan. Berkeley, California: University of California Press, 1977. 246p.
A collection of fifteen short articles by one of France's most distinguished mediaevalists. The volume is particularly good on such topics as the evolution of knighthood, the noble family, and the ideals of chivalry. One reviewer has called the articles collected here 'both a summary and the point of departure of current research' on the mediaeval aristocracy.

Renaissance

66 **Society in crisis: France in the sixteenth century.**
J. H. M. Salmon. New York: St. Martin's Press, 1975. 383p. bibliog.
A study of 16th century France that concentrates on the Wars of the Huguenots, 1562-98, a segment of French history the importance of which, the author feels, has been neglected. His aim is to achieve 'a reasonably comprehensible social and institutional history of sixteenth-century France', by focusing on the causes, campaigns, and conclusions of these wars and the social, institutional, economic, and political changes that accompanied them.

67 **France in the 16th century: a medieval society transformed.**
Donald Stone. Englewood Cliffs, New Jersey: Prentice-Hall, 1969. 180p. bibliog. (French Literary Background series).
Politically, the most important transformation that took place in 16th century France was the consolidation of the influence of the crown, a step which led to the absolute monarchy of the 17th century. This book is a good introduction to this process, concentrating on central royal figures such as Francis I, Catherine de Medici, and Henri IV, and the parts they played in strengthening the monarchy. The book is also a superior study of the culture and literature of the period, which are sensitively related to political developments.

68 **A time of glory: the Renaissance in France, 1488-1559.**
Anne Denieul-Cormier, translated from the French by Anne Fremantle, Christopher Fremantle. Garden City, New York: Doubleday; London: Allen & Unwin, 1969. 328p. map. bibliog. (U.K. edition has the title *The Renaissance in France*).
A well-illustrated volume that succeeds in capturing the richness of life in the French Renaissance. Basically a social history that discusses both events and personalities, the book is especially good on printing and travel during this period.

History. Seventeenth century

69 French humanism, 1470-1600.
Edited by Werner L. Gundetscheimer. New York: Harper & Row, 1969. 268p. bibliog. (Stratum series).

A collection of essays by scholars and historians on humanism and the culture of the French Renaissance. The first section of the book is an overview of interpretations of humanism in France; succeeding chapters relate this intellectual movement to various aspects of French culture, among them the printed book, Christianity, and the arts.

70 Life in Renaissance France.
Lucien Febvre, translated and edited by Marian Rothstein. Cambridge, Massachusetts: Harvard University Press, 1977. 163p. bibliog.

A welcome translation into English of a book by Lucien Febvre, perhaps the most influential 20th century French historian. The five essays included in this volume are good examples of Febvre's historiography, his emphasis on grasping a past reality in sharp, concrete detail. The articles also make an important contribution to knowledge of the French Renaissance which, as the preface to this book notes, 'has remained, stubbornly, the least understood part of French history'.

71 Introduction to modern France, 1500-1640; an essay in historical psychology.
Robert Mandrou, translated from the French by R. E. Hallmark. New York: Holmes & Meier, 1975. 285p. maps. bibliog.

A very interesting book by a French historian who is a follower of Lucien Febvre. This is a study of 'the collective mentality' of 16th century France. The author attempts to 'realize again the universe, the whole physical, intellectual, and moral universe [of the period]'. Thus, he delineates how 16th century man viewed his own body and his mind; he studies the forms that routine, cultural, and spiritual activities took; and he scrutinizes the routes of 16th century escapism into the realms of witchcraft and death.

Seventeenth century

72 Early modern France, 1560-1715.
Robin Briggs. New York: Oxford University Press, 1977. 242p. bibliog.

Briggs draws on the *Annales* school of French historians for the conceptions that underlie his treatment of the development of absolute monarchy in France during the later 16th and the 17th centuries. Although he excludes the cultural milieu, he identifies and links changes in the social, economic, and political areas during this period. The book is scholarly but readable. The bibliography comments on and evaluates the sources available to the historian.

History. Seventeenth century

73 **An introduction to seventeenth-century France.**
John Lough. New York: D. McKay, 1961. New ed. 291p. bibliog.

An excellent starting point for the study of France, 1600-1715, whether one is interested in the politics, the society, or the literature of these years. The author links these three spheres in a lucid presentation that covers the age and the setting; the towns, trade and industry; the nobility; the clergy; the development of absolutism, 1600-61; the height of absolutism, 1661-85; the writer and his public; language and literature; and the years of decline, 1685-1715.

74 **The Sun King.**
Nancy Mitford. New York: Harper & Row, 1966. 255p. bibliog.

The inclusion of this book marks a departure from the principles upon which this bibliography is compiled. However, if any individual symbolizes France, it is Louis XIV. This is a magnificently illustrated, very well-written history of *le Roi Soleil* and his reign. The author deftly captures the spirit and brilliance of the court at Versailles.

75 **The splendid century: some aspects of life in the reign of Louis XIV.**
W. H. Lewis. Garden City, New York: Doubleday, 1957. 304p. (Doubleday Anchor Books, A122).

A book that remains deservedly in print twenty years after it was first published, this is an engrossing account of the social and cultural life of the 17th century. The author covers the court and the king, the peasants, the church, the army, the country gentleman, the town, the medical world, the art of living, the galleys, sea travel, female education, and the world of letters. Readers who enjoy this book may wish to follow it with its sequel, Lewis's *Sunset of the splendid century* (London: Eyre & Spottiswoode, 1955).

76 **The impact of absolutism in France: national experience under Richelieu, Mazarin, and Louis XIV.**
Edited by W. F. Church. New York: Wiley, 1969. 195p. bibliog.

According to this book, the difficulty that faced France in the 17th century was 'the problem of social unrest'. The answer that France found for this problem was absolutism - the imposition of centralized government control. The primary sources and critical commentary collected here enable the student to evaluate whether or not the answer was the correct one. A lengthy bibliographical essay appended to the text lists further French and English sources that have bearing on the issue.

77 **France in the age of Louis XIII and Richelieu.**
Victor L. Tapie, translated from the French and edited by D. McN. Lockie. New York: Praeger, 1975. 622p. maps. bibliog.

A complete and unabridged translation of the second edition of this work, published in France in 1967 and regarded as the best one-volume treatment of the complex events of Richelieu's ministry and the Thirty Years' War. The trans-

History. Modern France-General, 1715 to the present

lation is excellent, and the translator is also to be commended for the annotated bibliography of English-language books on the period that he has added to the volume.

Modern France-General, 1715 to the present

78 **France in modern times: 1760 to the present.**
Gordon Wright. Chicago, Illinois: Rand McNally, 1960.
621p. maps. bibliog. (Rand McNally History series).
This history of modern France can be highly recommended: the author not only traces the main strands and trends of the period, but ably presents differing interpretations of events as well. Each section of the book is followed by a bibliographical chapter that discusses and evaluates the historiography of an era of French experience: the Enlightenment and revolutionary France, 1760-1814; France in search of a new equilibrium, 1814-1870; the rooting of the Republican spirit, 1870-1919; and contemporary France, an era of crisis, 1919-1960.

79 **France since the Revolution.**
Donald J. Harvey. New York: Macmillan, 1968. 366p. bibliog.
Since 1789 there have been five republics, two empires, and several constitutional monarchies in France. Harvey organizes his account of French history around the nation's search for a stable political order, but without neglecting social and economic factors.

80 **A history of modern France.**
Alfred Cobban. New York: Braziller, 1965. New ed., revised and enlarged. 3 vols. in 1. maps. bibliog.
An erudite and elegantly written introduction to the period of French history that began with the death of Louis XIV in 1715 and ended with the commencement of the De Gaulle régime in 1958. In addition to the 3-volumes-in-1 Braziller edition, the book is available in a more portable separate-volume paperback format (Harmondsworth, England; Baltimore, Maryland: Penguin Books, 1966). Volume I: *The Old Régime and the Revolution, 1715-1799*; Volume II: *From the First Empire to the Second Republic, 1799-1871*; Volume III: *France of the Republics, 1871-1958*. An excellent critical and evaluative bibliography is appended to each volume.

81 **France since 1789.**
Paul A. Gagnon. New York: Harper & Row, 1964. 560p. maps. bibliog.
An interpretative history of modern France, 1789 to the 1960s. The presentation is organized in terms of political régimes, with analyses of economic, social, religious, intellectual, and cultural matters. The author writes that his aim is 'to

History. Eighteenth century

invite a dialogue, a continuing debate, over judgments and interpretations of this complicated material'.

82 **The French nation from Napoleon to Pétain, 1814-1940.**
D. W. Brogan. New York: Harper, 1957. 328p.
Two adjectives reappear constantly in relation to the work of D. W. Brogan: 'indispensable' and 'idiosyncratic'. This narrative of French history from the Restoration to the end of the Third Republic is a good place for the reader to sample Brogan's style while learning about a complex period.

83 **French society and culture since the old régime.**
Edited by Evelyn M. Acomb, Marvin L. Brown. New York: Holt, Rinehart, & Winston, 1966. 296p. bibliog. (2nd Franco-American Colloquium, Greenville, Delaware, 1964).
A collection of scholarly essays on economic, political, cultural, and social developments in France since 1789. The twelve essays are grouped under four headings: 'Economic and social developments in France since the Old Régime'; 'Liberalism, Christianity and the Revolution of 1848'; 'The French image of Russia and Russian views of France'; and 'France and the Second World War'.

Eighteenth century

84 **An introduction to eighteenth-century France.**
John Lough. London: Longman, 1960. 349p. bibliog.
Were one asked to choose a starting point for the study of modern France, the last chapter of this book, 'Birth of modern France', could be suggested. It is a concise summary of the forces that make the difference between modern and traditional France, and it outlines the struggle between these forces - a battle that may just now have reached its conclusion in post-De Gaulle France. The book follows the plan of the author's *Introduction to seventeenth-century France* (q.v.), linking political, social, and cultural affairs in the seventy-four years between the death of Louis XIV in 1715 and the meeting of the *États Généraux* in 1789. Covers the peasantry; the towns; trade and industry; the privileged orders, clergy and nobility; the regent and Fleury, 1715-43; Louis XV, 1743-74; Louis XVI and Marie Antoinette; the writer and his public; and literature and ideas.

85 **The bourgeoisie in 18th-century France.**
E. G. Barber. Princeton, New Jersey: Princeton University Press, 1955. 165p. bibliog.
A study of the class upon which the interpretation of the French Revolution has centred. The author holds that the bourgeoisie were not dissatisfied with the inequality of 18th century French society so long as their upward mobility seemed possible. It was only after their ascent of the social scale appeared threatened that they adopted egalitarianism.

History. Eighteenth century

86 **The coming of the French Revolution, 1789.**
Georges Lefebvre, translated from the French by R. R. Palmer. Princeton, New Jersey: Princeton University Press, 1947. Reprinted, 1967. 233p.

Lefebvre may very well be the greatest historian of the French Revolution. In this book he has written for the general public, incorporating the findings of his more specialized works. What emerges is a well-rounded portrayal of the last years of the *ancien régime* to October 1789.

87 **The French prerevolution, 1787-1788.**
Jean Egret, translated from the French by Wesley D. Camp. Chicago, Illinois: University of Chicago Press, 1977. 314p. bibliog.

The first complete English translation of the standard French work on the 1787-88 'revolt of the nobles', which preceded the Revolution of 1789. The author covers the first and second Assemblies of Notables and the *parlements*.

88 **French Revolution.**
Francois Furet, Denis Richet, translated from the French by Stephen Hardman. New York: Macmillan; London: Weidenfeld & Nicolson, 1970. 416p. bibliog.

First published in 1965, this is the first recent French textbook history of the Revolution to abandon the Marxist interpretation of the event. A readable survey, it is well illustrated and has a short but valuable bibliographical essay which lists both French and foreign writings that are either landmarks in the historiography of the era or new approaches to the period.

89 **The French Revolution: conflicting interpretations.**
Edited by Frank A. Kafker, James M. Laux. New York: Random House, 1968. 344p. bibliog.

The selections included in this anthology of writings on the French Revolution were chosen for variety rather than consensus; thus, the student can use this book as an index to the opinions held by historians on various phases of the event. The bibliography appended to the book is well organized and should prove useful to anyone wishing to continue reading in this area.

90 **The French Revolution and Napoleon collection at Florida State University: a bibliographical guide.**
Donald D. Horward. Tallahassee, Florida: Friends of the Florida State University Library, 1973. 462p.

Students of the 1789-1815 era will be grateful for the publication of this catalogue of Florida State University's Stozier Library collection of 5,000 titles on the Revolution, Consulate, and Empire. The work is very well done - accurate and up to date. The unannotated entries are arranged alphabetically; subject access is through the index.

History. Eighteenth century

91 **The present state of French Revolutionary historiography, Alfred Cobban and beyond.**
John F. Cavanaugh. *French Historical Studies*, vol. 7, pt. 4 (Fall 1972), p. 587-606.
Required reading for history students, this article summarizes the directions that the historiography of the French Revolution has taken since Alfred Cobban revised the orthodox Marxist class struggle interpretation. The author reviews post-Cobban literature and notes that the revisionist view has now reached the textbook level with Furet and Richet's *History of the French Revolution* (q.v.). The author points out several areas in which historical research remains to be done, mentioning in particular the lack of writing on the pre-revolutionary régime.

92 **The French Revolution.**
A. Mathiez, translated from the French by Catherine A. Phillips. New York: Knopf, 1928. 509p. Reprinted, New York: Russell, 1962.
Mathiez, who died in 1932, was one of the most influential historians of the Revolution, developing what Gordon Wright calls 'the radical or common-man interpretation' of the event, a theory that has influenced many scholars. This book covers the Revolution to 1794 and depicts Robespierre as the hero of the era.

93 **The French Revolution.**
Georges Lefebvre, translated from the French by E. M. Evans, J. H. Stewart, J. Friguglietti. New York: Columbia University Press, 1962-64. 2 vols. bibliog.
A competent translation of a classic work. Volume I: The French Revolution from its origins to 1793; Volume II: The French Revolution from 1793 to 1799.

94 **The French Revolution and Napoleon; with a new annotated bibliography.**
Leo Gershoy. New York: Appleton-Century-Crofts, 1964. 584p. maps. bibliog.
An account of France from the collapse of the *ancien régime* to the fall of Napoleon. Gershoy's book is often recommended as the starting point for study of the period. His orderly and remarkably complete 584-page presentation is further enhanced by the 34-page bibliography - a full listing of works on the period that covers historiography, bibliography, sources and reference works, general accounts, background studies, and studies on administrative, political, social, economic, and intellectual aspects.

95 **The French Revolution.**
M. J. Sydenham. New York: Putnam, 1965. 255p. bibliog.
Drawing on recent scholarship the author, who also wrote an important study of the Girondins (*The Girondins*, q.v.), centres this general history on what he considers the central feature of the Revolution: 'the emergence of the new religion of nationalism, and the attempt to reconcile constitutional authority with popular control of power'.

History. Eighteenth century

96 **The French Revolution: a concise history.**
Norman Hampson. London: Thames & Hudson, 1975. 192p. bibliog.

Hampson states in his preface that his book is 'a personal statement rather than a digest of accepted opinion...intended for the layman who enjoys reading history'. As such, emphasis is placed on the roles played by individuals in the Revolution. Abundant illustrations - reproductions of Revolutionary cartoons, paintings, and posters - add a visual dimension to the narrative. This book is a good starting point for the nonacademic reader.

97 **The era of the French Revolution, 1789-1799: ten years that shook the world.**
Leo Gershoy. Princeton, New Jersey: Van Nostrand, 1957. 192p. bibliog. (Anvil Books, no. 22).

A concise summary of the Revolution, organized according to the three political régimes of the revolutionary decade: the Constitutional Monarchy, 1789-92; the Jacobin Commonwealth, 1792-94; the Constitutional Republic, 1795-99.

98 **A decade of revolution, 1789-1799.**
Crane Brinton. New York: Harper & Row, 1934. Reprinted, 1963. 330p. maps. bibliog. (The Rise of Modern Europe).

A book that is a well-written and reliable overview of the ten years of the Revolution from the monarchical experiments of 1789 to the 18th of Brumaire. The author covers more than the political history of this tumultuous era: he includes social and economic developments, religious trends, and has a particularly good chapter on the arts and sciences. Appended to the narrative is a critical bibliographical essay on the historiography of the Revolution to 1934. This is recommended to those readers who wish for an introduction to the early classics of revolutionary historiography: Taine, Aulard, Mathiez, and Gaxotte.

99 **A short history of the French Revolution, 1789-1799.**
Albert Soboul, translated from the French by Geoffrey Symcox. Berkeley, California: University of California Press, 1977. 171p. bibliog.

This recent translation of *La révolution française* makes more of the work of an influential French Marxist historian available to the English-reading public. The book is a convenient summation of the author's interpretation of the Revolution in the classic Marxist tradition of class struggle, bourgeoisie versus nobility.

100 **Twelve who ruled: the year of the Terror in the French Revolution.**
R. R. Palmer. Princeton, New Jersey: Princeton University Press, 1974. Reprinted, 1959. 417p. bibliog.

The twelve were Bertrand Barère, Jean-Nicolas Billaud-Varenne, Lazare Carnot, Jean-Marie Collot d'Herbois, Georges Couthon, Marie-Jean Herault de Sechelles, Robert Lindet, Prieur of the Côte-d'Or, Prieur of the Marne, Maximilien Robespierre, André Jeanbon Saint-André, Louis-Antoine Saint-Just - the members of the Committee of Public Safety who ruled France from September 1793 until the

History. Eighteenth century

9th of Thermidor of the Year II. This book is considered the definitive study of the year of the Reign of Terror. An epilogue traces the survivors after the 9th of Thermidor.

101 **Paris in the Terror: June, 1793-July, 1794.**
Stanley Loomis. Philadelphia, Pennsylvania: Lippincott, 1964. 415p. bibliog.

A popular account of the Reign of Terror that complements Palmer's scholarly tome (previous item). A vivid narration of the same blood-drenched period, the book begins with Charlotte Corday's assassination of Marat on 13 July 1793, and ends with the execution of Robespierre a year later.

102 **The Jacobins: an essay in the new history.**
Crane Brinton. New York: Macmillan, 1930. 319p. bibliog. Reprinted, New York: Russell, 1961.

Although written in 1930, this study of the Jacobins remains a basic text for the student of the Revolution. Brinton describes his book as a work of 'retrospective sociology' that seeks to extract a 'Jacobin' and 'Jacobinism' from the words and deeds of the ordinary members of the Society of Friends of the Constitution. Chapters detail the clubs' organization, membership, tactics, platforms, ritual, and faith.

103 **The social origins of the French Revolution: the debate on the role of the middle classes.**
Edited by Ralph W. Greenlaw. Lexington, Massachusetts: Heath, 1975. 259p. bibliog. (Problems in European Civilization).

A book that can serve as a guide through one of the most disputed areas in the interpretation of the Revolution. The editor's introduction surveys, summarizes, and comments on the conflicting opinions held by various historical schools on the exact role of the bourgeoisie in the Revolution. The body of the volume gives excerpts from the writings of scholars of differing viewpoints. An excellent bibliography is included for those who might wish to pursue the subject.

104 **The Girondins.**
M. J. Sydenham. London: University of London, Athlone Press, 1961. 252p. bibliog. (University of London Historical Studies, 8).

Alfred Cobban called this work 'a major reinterpretation of revolutionary politics, which demolishes the legend of a great Girondin party'. An important book that corrects an unbalanced picture of Revolutionary politics. The author reviews the theories that have been suggested about the Girond by historians, considers the trial records of Girondin leaders, and 'attempts to ascertain the origins, the real nature, and the ultimate extent of the supposed party by the examination of developments 1791-1792'.

History. Nineteenth century

105 **Napoleon: for and against.**
P. Geyl. New Haven, Connecticut: Yale University Press, 1949. 477p. maps.
A staggering amount of material has been written on Napoleon. This book is a good way into the literature: it presents the differences in opinion on the various aspects of Bonaparte's career, centring on the major question of whether he consolidated or destroyed the Revolution.

106 **Napoleon and the awakening of Europe.**
F. M. H. Markham. London: English Universities Press, 1954. 183p. (Teach Yourself History Library). Reprinted, Mystic, Connecticut: Verry, 1972.
A short reexamination of some beliefs about the first Emperor of the French. The author disagrees with the view that Napoleon was the first modern dictator, seeing him rather as the last in the line of enlightened despots of the 18th century.

Nineteenth century

107 **Conflicts in French society: anticlericalism, education, and morals in the nineteenth century; essays.**
Edited by Theodore Zeldin. London: Allen & Unwin, 1970. 236p. map. bibliog. (St. Antony's College, Oxford. Publications, no. 1).
The thread that ties these essays together is the repercussions in everyday life of the struggle between Christianity and secularism in 19th century France. The essays centre on clashes between the values of the two systems as they occurred in the home, the school, and in local politics. The subject is perceptively treated and the reader will derive many fresh insights from this work.

108 **The revolutionary movement in France, 1815-1871.**
J. P. Plamenatz. London: Longmans Green, 1952. 184p. bibliog.
This presentation of one aspect of 19th century French history views the 1815-71 period as filled with movements that considered themselves 'the spiritual posterity of the great revolution and wish to destroy the monarchy'. According to the author, these groups were united by their 'common hostility to the friends of privilege, authoritarian government, and the church'. Whether or not one agrees with this interpretation of 19th century revolutions, one will find in this book a close account of revolutionary events from the Restoration to the establishment of the Third Republic.

27

History. Nineteenth century

109 The rebellious century, 1830-1930.
Charles Tilly, Louise Tilly, Richard Tilly. Cambridge, Massachusetts: Harvard University Press, 1975. 354p. bibliog.

The authors use statistical evidence to write a history of 'collective violence' in France, Italy, and Germany during the one hundred years extending from 1830 to 1930. The seventy-page chapter on France outlines the 'repertoire' of French violence, analysing riots, strikes, class struggles, and mass revolutions. 19th and 20th century patterns of power, politics, wealth, and organization are compared and contrasted.

110 The French Revolution of 1830.
David H. Pinkney. Princeton, New Jersey: Princeton University Press, 1972. 397p. bibliog.

The revolution that began in July 1830 has never received the attention from historians accorded its predecessor of 1789 or its successor of 1848. Readers, then, will be grateful to the author for this up-to-date presentation, based on original research.

111 The French Second Republic: a social history.
Roger Price. Ithaca, New York: Cornell University Press, 1972. 386p. bibliog.

An informative account of the Revolution of 1848 and the Second Republic, provocative in the challenge it offers - by means of statistical analysis - to the Marxist interpretation of the 1848 events. Price analyses the structure of crisis-ridden mid-19th century society and social conditions in 1847, then traces the course of events from February 1848 to the coup d'état of 1851.

112 Revolution and reaction: 1848 and the Second French Republic.
Edited by Roger Price. London: Croom Helm; New York: Barnes & Noble, 1975. 333p. bibliog.

A companion volume to its editor's *French Second Republic: a social history* (previous item), this book is a collection of articles on the political history of the period covered in the earlier publication. A seventy-two-page interpretative introductory essay by Price ties the articles together.

113 Education and change in a village community: Mazières-en-Gatine, 1848-1914.
Roger Thabault, translated from the French by Peter Tregear. New York: Schocken, 1971. 270p. maps. bibliog.

A study of the social history of a French village that emphasizes the role played by the village school in both transforming and stabilizing the local social order.

History. Nineteenth century

114 **France, 1848-1945.**
Theodore Zeldin. New York; Oxford, England: Oxford University Press, 1973-77. 2 vols. (Oxford History of Modern Europe).
A book that one cannot recommend too highly. Based on exhaustive scholarship - the culmination of twenty-one years of research - and written with wit and vigour. The author achieves his aim of clarifying, without simplifying, the complex levels of French social and historical reality - ideological, institutional, and emotional. Volume I is entitled 'Ambition, love and politics'; Volume II, 'Intellect, taste, and anxiety'. This work is the point of departure for anyone seriously interested in this period of French history.

115 **The development of modern France, 1870-1939.**
D. W. Brogan. New York: Harper & Row, 1966. Rev. ed. 2 vols. (Harper Torchbooks; The Acameny Library).
An authoritative treatment of the history of the Third Republic by a distinguished British historian, writing for the general public. He concentrates on the political history, rather than the social history, of the era.

116 **The Paris Commune of 1871.**
Frank Jellinek. New York: Oxford University Press, 1937. 447p. bibliog.
In this study of the Paris Commune, Jellinek presents events and facts in a Marxist framework. In order to gain perspective, the reader should balance his account against that given from a liberal viewpoint in Edward Mason's *The Paris Commune: an episode in the history of the socialist movement* (New York: Macmillan, 1930), or the more recent study of Alistair Horne (see next item).

117 **The fall of Paris, the siege and the Commune, 1870-71.**
Alistair Horne. New York: St. Martin's Press, 1966. 458p. maps. bibliog.
The author avoids interpretations and gives a lengthy, detailed, and impartial account of the facts pertaining to the Franco-German War, the siege of Paris and the Commune. This is the first volume in the author's trilogy on what he des cribes as 'the lethal course of Franco-German relations over the past century'.

118 **France, 1870-1914: politics and society.**
R. D. Anderson. London: Routledge, 1977. 224p. bibliog.
A thorough analysis of political interaction in the pre-First World War Third Republic. The book deals with such topics as the distribution of political power among the social classes; the manipulation of power in Parliament; the influence of political leadership; the development of political movements and pressure groups; and the foreign and colonial policies of republican France. The author is to be commended for his grasp of the ambiguities inherent in the last subject. An appendix giving details of Third Republic elections and governments adds to the value of the book, as does an annotated bibliography.

History. Twentieth century

119 **The decline of French patriotism, 1870-1940.**
Herbert Tint. London: Weidenfeld & Nicolson, 1964. 272p. bibliog.

The author ably combines social, political, and psychological insights in this 'history of patriotic attitudes'. Discusses Gambetta, Deroulède and the *Ligue des Patriotes*, Boulanger, Taine, Renan, Barrès, the Dreyfus case, Peguy, *Action Française*, Bolshevism, and fascism in relation to the challenges and crises of patriotism in the French mentality.

120 **The Dreyfus case: a reassessment.**
Guy Chapman. New York: Reynal, 1955. 400p. bibliog.

The Dreyfus affair tore apart the fabric of French life in 1897-99. Of the many books written on the subject, this can be cited as an accessible narration. The volume is illustrated with photographs, and an appendix gives a selection of the critical documents of the case, a calendar of events, and a bibliography.

Twentieth century

121 **The nationalist revival in France, 1905-1914.**
Eugen Weber. Berkeley, California: University of California Press, 1959. Reprinted, 1968. 237p. bibliog.

Nationalism experienced a revival in France in the decade prior to the First World War. Weber, the historian of the *Action Française*, is well qualified to place the movement in proper perspective: his purpose is 'to identify the phenomenon and to try to understand the connection of nationalism and patriotism in its make-up'. He has 'tried to provide a useful, accurate picture of the changing temper of the country and, especially, of the opinions and actions of the politically significant men or groups'.

122 **The price of glory: Verdun, 1916.**
Alistair Horne. London: Macmillan, 1962; New York: St. Martin's Press, 1963. 371p. bibliog.

A detailed military history of the battle that marked the end of Germany's chance of winning the First World War. Based on published sources.

123 **The collapse of the Third Republic: an inquiry into the fall of France in 1940.**
William L. Shirer. New York: Simon & Schuster, 1969. 1082p. maps. bibliog.

Shirer, an eyewitness to the French military disaster of May-June 1940, has not only written a detailed account of those days, but a history of the Third Republic as well. He chronicles its rise (1871-1919); the illusions and realities of its triumphant years (1919-34); its decline (1934-39); and the chaos of its defeat and collapse (1939-40).

History. Twentieth century

124 **The week France fell.**
Noel Barber. New York: Stein & Day, 1976. 321p. maps.
A close account, based on memoirs and personal interviews with participants, of the events of the week that began Monday, 10 June 1940, and ended on Sunday, 16 June. A vivid reconstruction of these days, for those who wish to capture an 'on-the-spot' feeling.

125 **The war in France and Flanders, 1939-1940.**
Major L. F. Ellis. London: H.M. Stationery Office, 1953. 425p. (History of the Second World War. U.K. Military Series).
A book considered to be an excellent account of the 1940 campaign and the French military disaster. Another fine book on the subject is Major-General Sir Edward Spears' two-volume *Assignment to catastrophe* (New York: A. A. Wyn, 1954-55).

126 **Strange defeat.**
Marc Bloch, translated from the French by Gerard Hopkins. London, New York: Oxford University Press, 1949. 178p. Reprinted, New York: Octagon, 1967.
The author was, of course, an outstanding mediaevalist and professor of economic history at the Sorbonne. He was also a captain in the French army and as such took part in the 1940 campaign. In this little book - often cited as the best short account of the fall of France - Bloch, writing immediately after the event and from the viewpoint of a participant, probes the military, social, and intellectual failures of French leadership that led to the 1940 defeat.

127 **France, 1940-1955.**
Alexander Werth. New York: Holt, 1956. 764p. bibliog.
The author states in his introduction that his theme is 'France's place in the world, and all the political controversies and discussions that have, directly or indirectly, been connected with this question'. Covers the occupation years, the early De Gaulle period, the cold war, and the French in Indochina.

128 **France between the republics.**
Dorothy Pickles. London: Contact Publications, 1946. 247p.
On 10 July 1940 the French Parliament voted itself out of existence and the Third Republic expired. From that day until the Liberation five years later, France was ruled by those who sought to recast her institutions according to a system of ideas best described as a bizarre concoction of authoritarianism, paternalism, capitalism, nationalism, and fascism. This book gives a concise and factual description of the institutions in which the Vichy government sought to preserve its values and its view of social and economic relationships.

History. Twentieth century

129 **The Vichy regime, 1940-44.**
Robert Aron, in collaboration with Georgette Elgey, translated from the French by Humphrey Hare. London: Putnam, 1958. 536p. bibliog.

A translation and abridgment of the author's *Histoire de Vichy, 1940-1944* (Paris, 1955). This is a standard but not entirely satisfactory work on the Vichy government: the French government still withholds access to official Vichy papers, making a thorough account of the period an impossibility. This volume is based primarily on the trial records of Vichy leaders. It concentrates on the politics within the government and covers the régime from 12 June 1940 to 26 April 1945.

130 **Vichy France: old guard and new order, 1940-1944.**
Robert O. Paxton. New York: Knopf, 1972. 399p. bibliog.

The best history of Vichy to date. A solid, well-documented presentation, it covers more than the political history of the régime. The bibliographical note appended to the text discusses the problem of the unavailability of sources for the study of Vichy France.

131 **The French against the French: collaboration and resistance.**
Milton Dank. Philadelphia, Pennsylvania: Lippincott, 1974. 365p. bibliog.

A highly coloured, uncritical narrative of events in France under German occupation, 1940-44, when France, according to the author, 'was the only [country] in which collaboration with Hitler was official policy and in which tens of thousands of the occupied eagerly served the conqueror against their fellow countrymen'.

132 **The French resistance, 1940 to 1944.**
Frida Knight. London: Lawrence & Wishart, 1975. 242p. bibliog.

Frida Knight, a British national, was interned by the Germans in France, escaped, and was aided by the Resistance to reach England. Her book is a history of the anti-Nazi movement, beginning with early anti-fascist protests in 1934, covering the underground during the German Occupation and Vichy régime, and ending with the immediate political sequel to the Allied victory. The work contains a particularly interesting chapter, 'Culture in the Resistance'. A detailed calendar of events, 1933-45, is also helpful in following the history of the period.

133 **The night will end.**
Henri Frenay, translated from the French by Dan Hofstadter. New York: McGraw-Hill, 1976. 469p.

The recollections of Henri Frenay, who spent three years in the French underground movement before being called to London to serve on De Gaulle's National Liberation Committee. The book is particularly informative on the underground newspaper, *Combat*, and on the clandestine press and its operation during the Nazi occupation.

History. Twentieth century

134 The politics of resistance in France, 1940-1944.
John Sweets. DeKalb, Illinois: Northern Illinois University Press, 1976. 260p. bibliog.

An important contribution to the literature on the Resistance in France, the first book in English to study the politics within the movement. The study centres on the growth of the *Mouvements Unis de la Résistance* in southern France, but places it in the context of the entire Resistance. Readers will find this account of underground politics both intriguing and informative, and students of the period will at last have available factual details on the internal organizational structure of Resistance groups.

135 SOE in France: an account of the British Special Operations Executive in France, 1940-1944.
M. R. D. Foot. London: H.M. Stationery Office, 1976. New ed. 580p. maps. bibliog.

The British Special Operations Executive was organized shortly after the fall of France in 1940; its agents conducted secret anti-Nazi operations there until the war ended. The British government, concerned that there should be 'an accurate and dispassionate account' of its activities, commissioned this history and opened Foreign Office SOE papers to its author. The result is the most balanced and complete account possible at this date. It is also a fascinating and, in its understatement and objectivity, an impressive narration. An excellent discussion of sources and archives consulted in writing the book and an annotated bibliography of published memoirs and histories of the period follow the main text.

136 French politics: the first years of the Fourth Republic.
Dorothy Pickles. London: Royal Institute of International Affairs, 1953. 302p. bibliog.

This book covers the two years of the postwar provisional government and the first five years of the Fourth Republic, discussing both internal and foreign affairs. In the last quarter of the volume, 'A provisional balance-sheet', the author sums up, as far as possible, the situation in 1951 in regard to the working of the constitution, economic and social problems, and the parliamentary crises that plagued - and were to continue to plague - the Fourth Republic.

137 Modern France: problems of the Third and Fourth Republics.
Edited by E. M. Earle. Princeton, New Jersey: Princeton University Press, 1951. 522p. bibliog.

Postwar France - the 'New France' - has been the subject of several symposium studies by scholars and experts pooling their knowledge of diverse aspects of the nation. Although this volume is now nearly thirty years old, it is still worth reading for its well-presented analyses of France in a state of crisis. The contributors, mostly Americans, discuss social, economic, military, diplomatic, cultural, intellectual, and scientific affairs.

138 The Algerian insurrection, 1954-1962.
Edgar O'Ballance. Hamden, Connecticut: Archon Books, 1967. 231p. maps. bibliog.

A pro-French view of the course of events in Algeria, November 1954 to July 1962. In the author's opinion, 'the ultimate victory was not gained by conven-

History. Twentieth century

tional battle, such as that at Dien Bien Phu, but by political and diplomatic means'.

139 A savage war of peace: Algeria, 1954-1962.
Alistair Horne. New York: Viking Press, 1978. 604p. bibliog.

The author attempts in this book the difficult task of writing an objective history of the Algerian War, an assignment complicated by the unavailability of records - particularly the Algerian - and unsettled disputes over both facts and interpretations. What Horne has completed, based on the records to which he was given access and on personal interviews with participants in the conflict, can be regarded as the point of departure for future work.

140 The Algerian problem.
Edward Behr. London: Hodder & Stoughton, 1961. 256p.

Although this book was written before the end of the Algerian conflict and is thus incomplete, it remains a valuable account of the Algerian War. A more recent, well-documented account is Philippe Tripier's *Autopsie de la guerre d'Algérie* (Paris, 1972).

141 The French stake in Algeria, 1945-1962.
Tony Smith. Ithaca, New York: Cornell University Press, 1978. 224p. map.

A perceptive contribution to the current effort to write the history of and interpret the French role in North Africa. Smith, an American professor of political science, analyses the progress of French disengagement in North Africa from the end of the Second World War to the withdrawal from Algeria. In his view, the French had made heavy investments - economic, moral, strategic, and psychological - in Northern Africa, and were thus prevented from ever assessing the situation in a realistic way. The misguided policy followed in North Africa contributed to the downfall of the Fourth Republic.

142 The De Gaulle republic: quest for unity.
Roy C. Macridis, Bernard E. Brown. Homewood, Illinois: Dorsey Press, 1960. 400p. (Dorsey Series in Political Science). Reprinted, Westport, Connecticut: Greenwood Press, 1976.

A book written in 1959-60, as France entered the De Gaulle era, that gives an on-the-spot picture of the beginnings of the Fifth Republic. Narrates De Gaulle's coming to power, and discusses the new institutions, ideologies, political forms, and policies of his régime. A major part of the volume is devoted to an examination of the constitution of the Fifth Republic, which is reproduced in the appendix.

143 Europe against De Gaulle.
John Pinder. New York: Praeger, 1963. 160p.

The title of the book is explained in its preface as a call to arms: British writer Pinder sees De Gaulle as the representative of 'antique chauvinism', and contrasts his ideas and principles with those of Jean Monnet, whose plans for a European community he favours. Indeed, Pinder sees the struggle of the political forces

History. Twentieth century

represented by these men not only in terms of nationalism versus federalism, but in even larger terms of chaos against order. Now that both De Gaulle and Monnet are gone, this book has to be reassessed for relevance, but several of Pinder's points are well taken.

144 France.
Douglas Johnson. New York: Walker & Co., 1969. 271p. map. bibliog.

The major part of this competent presentation of 20th century French history examines De Gaulle and the Fifth Republic. In a chapter entitled 'Tour de France' Johnson speculates urbanely on the inexhaustible subject of French character and the changes that have taken place in the 'New France', making some interesting observations on French cultural symbols and the French sense of the past.

145 De Gaulle and the New France.
Peter Larmour. *Yale Review*, vol. 45, pt. 4 (Summer 1966), p. 500-20.

A good article that places De Gaulle in the historical context of modernization in France to explain some of the peculiarities of his domestic and foreign policies. The author makes sense of De Gaulle's style of leadership and policy of *la grandeur* by viewing the General as the Ataturk of France, who, like Ataturk or perhaps Nasser, took upon himself the task of weaning his people away from traditional ways of doing things and leading them into the modern world.

146 De Gaulle's legacy to Pompidou.
Stanley Hoffmann. *New Republic*, vol. 161, pt. 2 (12 July 1969), p. 19-21.

A summary of the eleven years of the De Gaulle régime by an expert on De Gaulle, France, and the Fifth Republic. In a second article, 'How will France change?' in the *New Republic* for 26 July 1969, Hoffman discusses France's post-De Gaulle future.

147 De Gaulle.
Brian Crozier. New York: Scribner's, 1973. 726p. bibliog.

A book that has been singled out by many reviewers as the best work now available on De Gaulle.

148 The French Fifth Republic: establishment and consolidation, 1958-1965; an annotated bibliography of the holdings at the Hoover Institution.
Grete Heinz, Agnes F. Peterson. Stanford, California: Hoover Institution Press, 1970. 170p. (Hoover Institution Bibliography Series, 44).

An excellent bibliography covering all the literature pertaining to the first seven years of the Fifth Republic in the collection of the Hoover Institution: books, pamphlets, leaflets, broadsides, government publications, and serials. The 2,234 entries are arranged alphabetically in two parts: non-serials in Part I, serials in Part II. Both French and English publications are included.

History. Twentieth century

149 **The French Fifth Republic: continuity and change, 1966-1970; an annotated bibliography.**
Grete Heinz, Agnes F. Peterson. Stanford, California: Hoover Institution Press, 1974. 125p. (Hoover Institution Bibliography Series, 54).
A sequel to the previous item, this work aims 'to complement and extend the first volume so as to encompass all documents available at the Hoover Institution on De Gaulle's Republic'. The 1,235 entries in in this volume are arranged on the same plan as those of the earlier publication.

150 **Decline or renewal? France since the 1930s.**
Stanley Hoffmann. New York: Viking Press, 1974. 529p. bibliog.
A collection of Hoffman's articles published between 1960 and 1974. The articles are organized into four sections: the Vichy régime; internal transformation of French society; France's attempt to find a new role in the world of superpowers; and the vision of Charles De Gaulle.

151 **The rise and fall of New France.**
G. M. Wrong. New York: Macmillan, 1928. 2 vols. bibliog. Reprinted, New York: Octagon, 1970.
This older book remains the standard account of France's overseas expansion during the Renaissance, and the conquest, consolidation, and finally the loss of her empire in North America. The author's detailed narrative traces the history of New France from the voyages of Jacques Cartier to the surrender of Quebec to the English.

152 **France and Britain in Africa: imperial rivalry and colonial rule.**
Edited by Prosser Gifford, William Roger Louis. New Haven, Connecticut: Yale University Press, 1971. 989p. maps. bibliog.
A massive scholarly work that focuses on Africa south of the Sahara - only three of the essays take North Africa as their subject. The volume includes a bibliographic essay by David Gardinier that provides a welcome guide to French writings on the colonial period.

153 **France and the Africans, 1944-1960: a political history.**
Edward Mortimer. London: Faber & Faber, 1964. 390p.
This straightforward account of the course of political events in Subsaharan Africa is a handy guide to the who, what, when, and where of French involvement there in the 1944-60 years. In spite of its title, the book does not cover Algeria, Tunisia, or Morocco. The author limits himself strictly to recounting facts and does not attempt interpretation.

History. Twentieth century

154 **Morocco under colonial rule: French administration of tribal areas, 1912-1956.**
Robin Bidwell. London: Cass, 1973. 349p. maps. bibliog.
This is not a general history of French rule in Morocco, but a specialized study that concentrates on the policy of the French towards Arab and Berber tribes. For a more comprehensive picture, the reader should consult Stephane Bernard's *Franco-Moroccan conflict, 1943-1956* (New Haven, Connecticut: Yale University Press, 1968).

155 **French colonialism in tropical Africa, 1900-1945.**
Jean Suret-Canale, translated from the French by Till Gottheimer. New York: Pica Press, 1971. 521p. bibliog.
A translation of volume 2 of the author's *Afrique noire: occidentale et centrale.* Suret-Canale's verdict on colonialism and French imperialism in Africa is largely negative. The book is scholarly, well documented, and based on French sources.

Folklore

156 **A book of the Basques.**
Rodney Gallup. Reno, Nevada: University of Nevada Press, 1930. Reprinted, 1970. 298p. map. bibliog.
This well-written survey of the Basques by an English folklorist surveys Basque history and culture with emphasis on folk songs, folk dances, literature and art forms. Some attention is paid to the Basque house, decoration, games and occupations. A chapter discusses the Basque language and the mystery of the origins of the Basques. New photographs have been taken for the reprinted edition.

157 **Breton folktales.**
Translated from the German by Ruth E. K. Meuss. London: G. Bell & Sons, 1971. 215p. bibliog.
Twelve folktales and eight legends from the Breton-speaking western half of Lower Brittany. Short notes give the sources of the tales.

158 **The Borzoi book of French folk tales.**
Edited by Paul Delarue, translated from the French by Austin Fife. New York: Knopf, 1956. 402p.
Fifty-four humorous tales, selected by Paul Delarue, a distinguished French folklore scholar best known for his compilation *Le Conte populaire français: catalogue raisonné des versions de France et des pays de langue française d'outremer.*

159 **Folktales of France.**
Edited by Geneviève Massignon, translated from the French by Jacqueline Hyland. Chicago, Illinois: University of Chicago Press, 1968. 315p. (Folktales of the World).
Folktales from the Pays de Retz, Brittany, Poitou, Marche, Angoumois and Ruffecois, Limousin, Massif Central, Forez, Franche-Comte, Dauphiné, Savoy, the Pyrenees, and Corsica. The editor was a scholar: her book is arranged for the student as well as the ordinary reader, with an index of motifs and an index of types of tales. In a very interesting introduction to the volume, Richard M.

Folklore

Dorson traces the history of the collection and study of folktales in France, from Charles Perault's *Contes de ma mère l'oye* in 1697 (incidentally, the first European book of folktales), to the modern work of Arnold van Gennep and Paul Delarue.

160 **French folk art.**
Jean Cuisenier, translated from the French by Thomas W. Lyman. Tokyo, New York: Kodansha, 1977. 310p. bibliog.

Perhaps the most comprehensive study of French folk art available in English, this volume's fifty-seven colour plates and 349 black-and-white photographs constitute an impressive record of traditional art in France.

Religion

161 **A literary history of religious thought in France.**
Henri Bremond, translated from the French by K. L. Montgomery. New York: Macmillan, 1928-1936. 3 vols. Reprinted, New York: Octagon, 1969.
An immense and erudite work on 17th century religious thought in France, written from a Catholic viewpoint. Volume 1 is entitled 'Devout humanism'; volume 2 is 'The coming of mysticism (1590-1620)'; and volume 3 is 'The triumph of mysticism'.

162 **Catholics and unbelievers in eighteenth century France.**
R. R. Palmer. Princeton, New Jersey: Princeton University Press, 1939. 236p. bibliog.
An evenhanded presentation of the ideas of those - most of whom were within the Church - who opposed the *philosophes* and the *Age des lumières*. The author discusses the thought of French Catholics from about 1740 to the Revolution largely in terms of its conflict with that of the unbelievers. He concludes that 'the orthodox of the eighteenth century offered an intelligent criticism of the philosophy of the Enlightenment', but the times were against them.

163 **French prophets of yesterday: a study of religious thought under the Second Empire.**
Albert L. Guerard. London: T. F. Unwin, 1913. 288p. bibliog.
An older work that is still valuable for its thorough exploration of the paths followed by Catholicism, Protestantism, Voltairianism, romantic humanism, and the scientific spirit in 19th century France.

Religion

164 Catholicism and crisis in modern France: French Catholic groups at the threshold of the Fifth Republic.
William Bosworth. Princeton, New Jersey: Princeton University Press, 1962. 407p. bibliog.

A sociological study that focuses on Catholic institutions and on the role of the Church as a political force in contemporary France. The author discusses the place of Catholic institutions in the laic republic and the social doctrine of the Church; he details the official ecclesiastical organization of the Church and examines Catholic social action groups, the Catholic press, and Catholic schools. He concludes his work with an interesting discussion of the philosophical framework upon which Catholic social action depends, and contrasts the Catholic viewpoint with those of other social reform and social revolutionary groups active in France. The book includes an excellent annotated bibliography.

165 The Catholic avant-garde: French Catholicism since World War II.
Jean-Marie Domenach, Robert de Montralon, translated from the French by Brigid Elson (and others). New York: Holt, 1967. 245p. bibliog.

This is a presentation of the views of the contemporary French Catholic Left through selections from the writings of its intellectuals, spiritual leaders, theologians, and priest-workers. Among the subjects treated are religious education, socialism, religious art, the priest-worker experiment, the Algerian War, and Christianity in rural life.

166 Church and state in France, 1300-1907.
Arthur Galton. London: E. Arnold, 1907. 290p. bibliog. Reprinted, New York: B. Franklin, 1972. (B. Franklin Research and Source Works Series. Selected Studies in History, Economics, and Social Sciences. N.S. 4(c) Modern European Studies).

This book was written shortly after the quarrel between the Third Republic and the papacy reached a climax in the Law of 9 December 1905, separating church and state in France. The author's presentation of the relations between the Roman Catholic Church and the French state begins with the origins of Gallicanism under Philip the Fair and continues through the 19th century. His viewpoint is urbane, if unsympathetic to the Church and the Roman Curia.

167 A history of Protestantism.
Emile G. Leonard, translated from the French by M. H. Joyce. London: Nelson, 1965. 3 vols. maps. bibliog.

This general history of Protestantism was addressed to the French public and is thus particularly strong in the history of the French Protestants. The first volume begins with the emergence and spread of Lutheranism and ends with Calvin; the second volume traces the movement from the end of the 16th century to the establishment and subsequent disestablishment of French Protestantism, and the last volume covers the era from the 18th century to the present.

Religion

168 **Witchcraft in France and Switzerland: the borderlands during the Reformation.**
E. William Monter. Ithaca, New York: Cornell University Press, 1976. 232p. bibliog.
This book on witchcraft in the Jura region is of interest because recent material on the phenomenon of witchcraft in France is not easy to find.

Philosophy and Intellectual Life

General

169 **Histoire des idées en France.** (History of ideas in France.)
Roger Daval. Paris: Presses Universitaires de France, 1962.
128p. (Que Sais-je? Le Point des Connaissance Actuelles, 593).

A swift survey of French thought in the broadest sense: ideas in science, metaphysics, religion, politics, economics, psychology, and social theory from the Renaissance to the 20th century. An accessible presentation of the dominant themes in French intellectual life.

170 **History of modern philosophy in France.**
Lucien Lévy-Bruhl. Chicago, Illinois: Open Court Publishing Company, 1899. 500p. bibliog. Reprinted, New York: B. Franklin, 1971.

A history of French philosophy in the 17th, 18th and 19th centuries that omits 'philosophers of lower rank and only moderate originality'. Included are Descartes and Cartesianism, Malebranche, Pascal, Bayle, Fontenelle, Montesquieu, Rousseau, Condillac, Condorcet, the Ideologists, Maine de Biran, Cousin, Comte, Renan, and Taine. Lévy-Bruhl states at the outset that his purpose in writing this book is to isolate the 'French' part of modern philosophy. In his final chapter he gives his findings, one of which is that there exists a close affinity between modern French philosophy and the mathematical spirit.

Philosophy and Intellectual Life. Eighteenth century

Eighteenth century

171 **The Enlightenment.**
Norman Hampson. Baltimore, Maryland; Harmondsworth, England: Penguin Books, 1968. 304p. (Pelican History of European Thought, 4).

A book that has been called 'the best short account [of the Enlightenment] available in English, well-constructed and well-informed'. In his interpretation of the intellectual, cultural, political, and social factors that contributed to the movement known as the Enlightenment, the author traces the West's abandonment of traditional values and ways of doing things and its attempt to construct new ones. He is a subtle analyst of the contradictions of the Enlightenment, and this book is a pleasure to read.

172 **The French Enlightenment.**
J. H. Brummfitt. London, New York: Macmillan, 1972. 176p. bibliog. (Philosophers in Perspective).

A brief but thorough history of the French Enlightenment. The work is directed towards the non-specialist and centres on the thought of major Enlightenment figures, although excluding Rousseau. The concepts of the period are concisely and capably presented.

173 **The anti-philosophers: a study of the *philosophes* in eighteenth-century France.**
R. J. White. New York: Macmillan, 1970. 175p. bibliog.

An approachable account of the 'philosophical' movement in France prior to the Revolution. White views the *philosophes* as the popularizers of the ideas of the 17th century, who translated these ideas into ordinary language and introduced them into everyday life, thus inaugurating the era of modern history.

174 **In search of humanity: the role of the Enlightenment in modern history.**
Alfred Cobban. New York: G. Braziller, 1960. 254p.

A book that views the Enlightenment from the perspective of the 20th century. The author, concentrating mainly on the movement in England and France, analyses the intellectual and moral revolution of the 18th century in terms of the modern world and its problems, holding that the *Age des lumières* was the last great creative age in moral and political thought. A book that has been called 'one of the best-argued defenses of Enlightenment liberalism'.

175 **The aesthetic thought of the French Enlightenment.**
Francis X. J. Coleman. Pittsburgh, Pennsylvania: University of Pittsburgh Press, 1971. 167p. bibliog.

As its author intended, this book fills a gap in the literature devoted to the thought of the French Enlightenment by studying the aesthetic aspect of the new philosophy. Coleman's treatment of the subject is excellent: he tracks down the assumptions - tacit or overt - upon which 18th century aesthetic theories were based. As might be expected, a large part of the volume discusses Diderot, but Coleman does not neglect such lesser-known aestheticians as Crousaz, Saint-

Philosophy and Intellectual Life. Eighteenth century

Evremond, Batteux, and Condillac, whose theories prove of considerable interest in understanding this facet of Enlightenment thought.

176 **The geometric spirit: the Abbé de Condillac and the French Enlightenment.**
Isabel F. Knight. New Haven, Connecticut: Yale University Press, 1968. 321p. bibliog. (Yale Historical Publications; Miscellany, 89).

This study, intended 'to illuminate the texture, inner structure, and half-acknowledged tensions of the Enlightenment', centres on Condillac, but is not limited to his thought alone. Knight has mastered her subject: she deftly traces the 'geometric spirit' as it manifested itself in the realms of psychology, linguistics, aesthetics, education, economics, and history, and she ably ties together the diverse strands of Enlightenment thought.

177 **French thought in the eighteenth century.**
Daniel Mornet, translated from the French by Lawrence M. Levin. New York: Prentice-Hall, 1929. 336p. Reprinted, Hamden, Connecticut: Shoestring Press, 1969.

This oft-cited classic of intellectual history surveys intellectual and ethical developments in France from 1700 to 1789. Mornet discusses how 17th century rationalistic thought and ideas drawn from experimental science combined to produce a new spirit in 18th century France. The book is also good on the sentimental movement and the diffusion of a moral code based on sentiment.

178 **The attack on 'feudalism' in eighteenth-century France.**
J. Q. C. Mackrell. Toronto: University of Toronto Press; London: Routledge & Kegan Paul, 1973. 215p. bibliog. (Studies in Social History).

This study of the concept of 'feudalism' clarifies the attitude of 18th century writers and intellectuals to the social problems of their time, and clears up some misconceptions on 18th century class relationships. Among the topics covered are feudalism in 18th century French historiography, feudalism in juristic thought, the relations between the nobility and business, humanitarian objections to feudalism, and the inutility of feudalism.

179 **The revolutionary mentality in France, 1793-94.**
Richard Cobb. *History*, no. 146, vol. 42 (Oct. 1957), p. 181-96.

An extremely interesting contribution to the study of the French Revolution, this article considers 'the personal attitudes of a hypothetical person, called for the sake of convenience the average revolutionary, towards the common events of everyday life in the revolutionary movement, between the summer of 1793 and the late summer of the following year'. Cobb does not portray the revolutionary as the follower of a clear political ideology, but presents his mental life rather as a conglomeration of 'attitudes, reactions, prejudices, [and] behavior in the face of given problems and given situations'.

Philosophy and Intellectual Life. Nineteenth century

Nineteenth century

180 **Secular religions in France, 1815-1870.**
D. G. Charlton. London, New York: Oxford University Press, 1963. 249p. bibliog.

The author comments in his preface that his book is intended to fill a gap in the study of 19th century French intellectual history by detailing the 'background of non-Christian philosophical ideas [which is] nowhere conveniently presented'. The spiritual and intellectual substitutes for Christianity that the 19th century developed are fully covered: the cult of science, social religions, occult and neo-pagan religions, and the cult of history and progress. The author is a scholar, but he writes here for the general reader as well as for the student of the period, and the non-specialist will find this work both enjoyable and informative.

181 **Modern French philosophy: a study of the development since Comte.**
J. A. Gunn. London: T. F. Unwin, 1922. 358p. bibliog.

An older, but still useful, history of philosophical thought in France from 1851 to 1921. The author defines the central issue of the time as that of the reconciliation of science and conscience, a question that develops into the problem of freedom. An appendix gives a helpful comparative table of the chief philosophical works published between 1851 and 1921 in France, Germany, England, and the U.S.A.

Twentieth century

182 **Contemporary French philosophy: a study in norms and values.**
Colin Smith. New York: Barnes & Noble, 1964. 266p. bibliog.

Although this is not a book for those who have no acquaintance with contemporary French philosophy, anyone who has received an introduction to the subject will find the author's presentation useful. It is Smith's contention that French philosophy from 1930 to 1964 was based on a dualism, and it is around dualistic themes that he organizes his material. This thematic organization clarifies some of the more abstruse aspects of the subject. Smith also avoids concentrating exclusively on the Sartre-Camus group: his discussion of lesser-known, academic philosophers gives the reader a better-rounded picture of the existentialist era.

183 **Philosophic thought in France and the United States: essays representing trends in contemporary French and American philosophy.**
Edited by Marvin Farber. Buffalo, New York: University of Buffalo Publications in Philosophy, 1950. 775p. bibliog.

The nineteen essays by philosophers, scholars, and critics that constitute the first part of this volume are an excellent presentation of the intellectual ferment that

Philosophy and Intellectual Life. Twentieth century

made postwar French philosophy so exciting. Among those of particular interest: 'Phenomenology in France' (Jean Henry); 'Existentialism in France since the Liberation' (Robert Campbell); 'Catholic philosophy in France' (Henry Dumery); and 'Knowledge and social criticism' (Henri Lefebvre). Selected bibliographies follow each essay.

184 **Appraisal of French anthropology.**
M. Barber. *Current Anthropology*, vol. 18 (Sept. 1977), p. 575-6.

This short article is a report on an international colloquium, 'The Present Situation and Future of Anthropology in France', held in Paris, 18-22 April 1977, under the auspices of the Centre National de la Recherche Scientifique and the École des Hautes Études en Sciences Sociales; it can be recommended for a concise summary of the state of French anthropology from an Anglo-Saxon viewpoint. Barber reports that, as might be expected, Lévi-Strauss continues to dominate the discipline, but notes that the most interesting new developments are Marxist-oriented work being done in economic anthropology.

185 **French Freud: structural studies in psychoanalysis.**
Edited by Jeffrey Mehlman. *Yale French Studies*, no. 48 (1972), p. 1-202.

This special issue of *Yale French Studies* is 'an attempt to make available in English for the first time key French texts on Freud'. The articles collected include essays by the leading figures in France's belated discovery of Freud and psychoanalysis: Jacques Lacan, Jacques Derrida, Jean La Planche, Serge Leclaire, and J. B. Pontalis. The editor provides a helpful introductory essay.

186 **Psychoanalytic politics: Freud's French Revolution.**
Sherry Turkle. New York: Basic Books, 1978.

The French acceptance of Freud and his theories was long delayed: Turkle's account of the belated introduction of Freudian ideas and psychoanalytic concepts into the mainstream of French intellectual life is both shrewd and amusing.

187 **French historical method: the *Annales* paradigm.**
Traian Stoianovich. Ithaca, New York: Cornell University Press, 1976. 260p.

One of the first books in English describing the methodology of the *Annales* school of historiography and tracing its development. There is a good review of this book by Bernard Bailyn in the *Journal of Economic History*, vol. 37 (Dec. 1977), p. 1028-34, in which he discusses the strengths and weaknesses of the *Annales* historians and provides some insights into the intellectual milieu within which history is written in France.

188 **The cultural revolution: notes on the changes in the intellectual climate of France.**
Michel Crozier. *Daedalus*, vol. 93, pt. 1 (Winter 1964), p. 514-42.

In the early 1960s, the author writes, a change occurred in the role played by intellectuals in French society, with intellectual authority losing the preeminence formerly accorded it. Crozier regards this change as signalling a fundamental social realignment, which may have serious consequences for France and Europe.

Philosophy and Intellectual Life. Twentieth century

189 **The many faces of French Marxism.**
Pradeep Bandyopadhyay. *Science and Society*, vol. 36, pt. 2 (Summer 1972), p. 129-57.

An article that is quite good at communicating the intellectual ambiance of Marxism in France. The author states that his aim is to correct the prevalent unbalanced view which links French Marxism only to certain literary groups or figures or to the French Communist Party and its political ambitions. To counteract this view, Bandyopadhyay traces the impact of Marxist thought on historiography, economics, linguistics, and literary criticism, indicating how Marxist theory has, to some extent, provided explanations for the human experiences and concerns studied in these disciplines.

190 **France's new philosophers.**
Roger Kaplan. *Commentary*, vol. 65, pt. 2 (Feb. 1978), p. 73-6.

This article on the 'group of young French writers who have turned against the Marxist inheritance which for the past twenty or thirty years has been the birthright of French intellectuals' focuses on the writings of Bernard-Henri Lévy (*Barbarism with a human face*) and André Glucksmann (*The cook and the maneater* and *The master thinkers*). Kaplan discusses the rejection of Marxist thought and the negative reassessment of a communist social option by these former radical leftists.

Social and Political Theory

191 **French utopias: an anthology of ideal societies.**
Edited by Frank E. Manuel, Fritzie P. Manuel. New York: Free Press, 1966. 426p. Reprinted, New York: Schocken, 1971. (Studies in Libertarian and Utopian Tradition).

Utopian ideas have occupied the minds of many French social theorists, intellectuals, philosophers, and writers. In this anthology, the authors gather together samples of the social visions of Frenchmen from Rabelais to Teilhard de Chardin. Those who find their interest in the subject kindled might enjoy reading Manuel's *Prophets of Paris* (New York: Harper & Row, 1965), in which he discusses the social thought of Turgot, Condorcet, Saint-Simon, Fourier, and Comte.

192 **French liberal thought in the eighteenth century: a study of political ideas from Bayle to Condorcet.**
Kingsley Martin. Boston, Massachusetts: Little, Brown, 1929. 313p. bibliog. (Library of European Political Thought).

A standard work on the movement of ideas in 18th century France that appears in many bibliographies. The author's aim is 'to discover what that social creed we have since learned to call liberalism meant to the eighteenth-century thinkers who formulated and popularized it'. Discusses the revolutionary creed of liberty, equality, and fraternity; the rights of the individual; the *philosophes*; the philosophy of common sense; utilitariansim; the influence of the British; the doctrine of natural rights; and the religion of progress.

Social and Political Theory

193 **French corporative theory, 1789-1948: a chapter in the history of ideas.**
Matthew H. Elbow. New York: Columbia University Press, 1953. Reprinted, New York: Octagon, 1966. (Studies in History, Economics, and Public Law, no. 577).

A historical and analytical account of French corporative theory, this book begins with a survey of theories current before 1870. It then traces corporative thought from 1870 to 1918, analyses corporatism between the two World Wars, and ends with a sketch of the theory in action under the Vichy government.

194 **The obstructed path: French social thought in the years of desperation, 1930-1960.**
Henry S. Hughes. New York: Harper & Row, 1968. 304p. bibliog.

Between 1930 and 1960 France faced a series of economic, ideological, diplomatic, military, and moral crises that impelled many of her intellectuals, writers, philosophers, and scholars to take up the role of social theorist. This book considers the social speculations of a diverse group of thinkers, beginning with Lucien Febvre and Marc Bloch and the new orientations in historiography of the *Annales* school, and ending with the anthropological work of Claude Lévi-Strauss. Chapters deal with the social aspects of the writings of Gabriel Marcel, Jacques Maritain, André Malraux, Roger Martin du Gard, Georges Bernanos, Antoine de Saint-Exupéry, Jean-Paul Sartre, Maurice Merleau-Ponty, Albert Camus, and Pierre Teilhard de Chardin. Both the general reader and the student will find this book informative.

195 **Contemporary French political thought.**
Roy Pierce. London, New York: Oxford University Press, 1966. 276p. bibliog.

An analysis of the political ideas of the six intellectuals whom the author believes to be the principal contributors to the immediate post-Second World War discussion of fundamental problems of politics in France: Emmanuel Mounier, Simone Weil, Albert Camus, Jean-Paul Sartre, Bertrand de Jouvenel, and Raymond Aron. The first chapter of the book surveys the political ideas current in the 1930s and 1940s; the second chapter is a collective biography of the six. Succeeding chapters discuss the political ideas of each and a bibliography lists their major political writings.

196 **Democracy in France since 1870.**
David Thomson. New York, London: Oxford University Press, 1969. 5th ed. 344p. bibliog. (Royal Institute of International Affairs series).

A book that has been revised periodically since its first publication in 1946, and is considered indispensable for achieving an understanding of the working of democracy in France. Covers the revolutionary tradition and the social bases of French democracy; the democratic instruments of the Third Republic; the political, economic, and social problems that weakened the political structure of the Third Republic; the open schism with democracy, 1940-44; and the experience of democracy in the Fourth and Fifth Republics. Thomson concludes from his study of the phenomenon that 'the meaning and development of democracy in France

Social and Political Theory

since 1870 has shown how, repeatedly, its working and its ideals have been influenced by nationalism'.

197 **French democracy.**
Valéry Giscard d'Estaing, translated from the French by Vincent Cronin. Garden City, New York: Doubleday; London: Collins, 1977. 126p. (UK edition is entitled *Towards a new democracy*).
The third president of the Fifth Republic sets forth his ideals, principles, and proposals for change in what he describes as 'a plan designed for France as an historical and social entity'. In his view, both Marxism and traditional liberalism are inadequate either to explain the current situation or to guide France in the future. He proposes an 'anthropocentric approach' to France's problems and a 'pluralistic democracy' as the correct form of political organization.

198 **The American challenge.**
Jean-Jacques Servan-Schreiber, translated from the French by Ronald Steel. New York: Atheneum, 1968. 291p.
A book that excited much comment when it was published in France in 1967. The author, the founder of *L'Express*, sets forth his view that Europe has to restore her autonomy or sink to becoming a subsidiary of the USA. The solution he proposes is 'discriminating Americanization', with Europe following America in her art of organization and her investment in human intelligence, while avoiding the grosser aspects of her culture.

199 **Marxism in modern France.**
George Lichtheim. New York: Columbia University Press, 1966. 212p. bibliog.
A perceptive and well-written analysis, concerned with the theoretical side of French Marxism. A good presentation of the role Marxist doctrine once played, and of the transformation of that role into the part it now plays in contemporary France. The author centres his study of the Marxist phenomenon on the decades preceding and following the Second World War, but although emphasis is placed on these years, he also draws perceptively on the history and experience of the 19th century French labour movement and its relation to Marxist doctrine. The bibliography gives the standard French sources for the study of Marxism in France.

200 **Existential Marxism in postwar France: from Sartre to Althusser.**
Mark Poster. Princeton, New Jersey: Princeton University Press, 1975. 415p. bibliog.
Poster characterizes the postwar period in France as one of 'profound reorientation and vitality in social theory'. His study traces the relationship of Marxism and existentialism in recent French social theory, holding that the convergence of these two doctrines in Sartre and the *Arguments* group established the beginnings of a social theory of the New Left. In a very interesting epilogue, Poster discusses the events of May-June 1968 from the perspective of existential Marxism.

Social and Political Theory

201 **The origins of modern leftism.**
Richard Gombin, translated from the French by Michael K. Paul. Harmondsworth, England: Penguin Books, 1975. 144p. (Pelican Books).

Gombin, a French writer, provides in this book an introduction to a new political and social theory of the Left, drawn largely from French sources. He describes modern leftism as the use of Marxist analysis to achieve a critique of Marxism-Leninism.

Social Class, Social Groups, and Social Change

202 **Modern Europe: an anthropological perspective.**
Robert Anderson. Pacific Palisades, California: Goodyear, 1973. 163p. bibliog.
Four essays on present-day France are included in this volume: a brief discussion of the upper class, a consideration of changes occurring in a peasant village in the French Alps, a look at politics in a small village near Paris, and an article on the Basques.

203 **The vanishing peasant: innovation and change in French agriculture.**
Henri Mendras, translated from the French by Jean Lerner. Cambridge, Massachusetts: MIT Press, 1970. 289p. bibliog. (MIT Studies in Comparative Politics).
A comprehensive work of rural sociology, intended to illuminate the historic roots of the process of change that has diminished the ranks of the French peasantry, as well as to present the current situation and to make some predictions for the future. The first part of the book is a general consideration of change and innovation in peasant societies; the second part concentrates on the French farmer, his enterprise and his social relations.

204 **Village in the Vaucluse.**
Laurence Wylie. Cambridge, Massachusetts: Harvard University Press, 1974. 3rd ed. 390p. map.
This perceptive description of a year spent by the author, his wife, and children in Peyrane, a rural commune in France, is required reading for those wishing to understand how French social relations work. Wylie's original field work was

Social Class, Social Groups, and Social Change

done in 1950-51. The 1974 third edition has an epilogue that brings the reader up to date on changes that have taken place in the village.

205 Peasants against politics: rural organizations in Brittany, 1911-1967.
Suzanne Berger. Cambridge, Massachusetts: Harvard University Press, 1972. 298p. bibliog.

The author studied two backward departments in Brittany - Côtes-du-Nord and Finistère - to find out why 'peasant participation in a wide range of rural associations appeared to have little effect on politics'. Her in-depth report on this situation reveals the problems faced by peasant organizations and their rural members in encounters with mainstream French society.

206 Pont-de-Monvert: social structure and politics in a French village, 1700-1914.
Patrice L. R. Higonnet. Cambridge, Massachusetts: Harvard University Press, 1971. 217p. bibliog.

A well-documented social history of a village of the Lozère in south central France. Emphasis is placed on changes in the village's class structure through two centuries.

207 Bus stop for Paris: the transformation of a French village.
Robert T. Anderson, Barbara Gallatin Anderson. Garden City, New York: Doubleday, 1965. 303p. bibliog.

The authors bring historical and anthropological research methods to bear on the process of modernization in Wissous, a small village near Paris.

208 Chanzeaux: a village in Anjou.
Edited by Laurence Wylie. Cambridge, Massachusetts: Harvard University Press, 1966. 383p. maps.

This book by Laurence Wylie and his students is 'the cooperative effort of eighteen authors to describe a small rural community in western France, a village in Anjou [where] even in the eight years the authors have know it there have been important changes. Yet Chanzeaux as a social entity, as a personality, seems to persist. The fundamental question is to see how Chanzeaux retains this personality and at the same time evolves within itself as well as with the rest of France'. The book covers the history, agriculture, population, and social organization of Chanzeaux. Of particular interest is the discussion of the role played by religion and politics in the lives of the Chanzeans.

209 The red and the white: report from a French village.
Edgar Morin, translated from the French by A. M. Sheridan-Smith. New York: Pantheon Books, 1970. 263p. maps. (Also published London: Allen Lane, 1971, under the title *Plodemet: report from a French village*). (Pantheon's Series of Reports from Villages Throughout the World).

Another sociological study of the modernization of a French village, this time from the viewpoint of a French sociologist who scrutinized the changes taking

Social Class, Social Groups, and Social Change

place in a Brittany *bourg*, and found that 'the radical opposition of the political parties which traditionally divided a small French village into two different worlds, has moderated in recent years, although its influence is still felt'.

210 The world of the office worker.
Michel Crozier, translated from the French by David Landau. Chicago, Illinois: University of Chicago Press, 1971. 224p. bibliog. (Studies of Urban Society).

In this book, the author uses sociological concepts to analyse the world view of the French white-collar worker. His discussion of the strategies and tactics utilized by the office worker to handle problems illuminates the mentality of middle-class Frenchmen and Frenchwomen. The reader should bear in mind, however, that the research upon which this book is based was carried out in 1957.

211 Elites in French society: the politics of survival.
Ezra N. Suleiman. Princeton, New Jersey: Princeton University Press, 1978. 296p.

An important contribution to the study of class relationships in French society. Suleiman looks at élite groups in both public and private sectors, examining the state institutions that produce the élite (particularly the *grandes écoles*), the organization of élites, and the political implications of an élitist system within a democracy. His analysis of the French élites' ability to legitimate themselves and their roles in the context of a democratic society is a valuable contribution to understanding French social structure.

212 Women in Europe since 1750.
Patricia Branca. New York: St. Martin's Press, 1978. 233p.

The focus in this book is primarily on women in France and England. The author examines the roles allotted to women in work, family, and society, and how women's public and private roles were integrated.

213 Women: roles and status in eight countries.
Edited by J. Z. Giele, A. C. Smock. New York: Wiley, 1977. 443p. bibliog.

This recent publication contains C. B. Silver's essay on women in contemporary France, 'France: contrasts in familial and societal roles'.

214 Old age in European society: the case of France.
Peter N. Stearns. New York: Holmes & Meier; London: Croom Helm, 1976. 163p.

The author chose France as his focus in this sociological history of the aged in a traditional culture because of the high proportion of elderly people in the French population. The result is an informative picture of how France deals with her aged.

Social Class, Social Groups, and Social Change

215 **Old people, new lives: community creation in a retirement residence.**
Jennie-Keith Ross. Chicago, Illinois: University of Chicago Press, 1977. 227p. bibliog.

The author applies sociological and anthropological methods and perspectives in her study of *retirées* in a French retirement residence in the Paris suburb of Bagnolet. Her focus is on conflicts and agreements in the creation of a viable community by the residents of *Les Floralies*.

216 **Drinking in French culture.**
Roland Sadoun, Giorgio Lolli, Milton Silverman. New Brunswick, New Jersey: Center of Alcohol Studies, 1965. 133p. bibliog. (Rutgers University. Rutgers Center of Alcohol Studies. Monographs, 5).

A sociological discussion of both the normal place of alcohol consumption in French society and of problems of excessive drinking. Chapters consider popular and medical attitudes towards alcohol, the general drinking patterns of the French, the drinking patterns of French alcoholics, and the prevention of alcoholism in France.

217 **Social welfare in France.**
Edited by Pierre Laroque, translated from the French by Philip Grant, Noel Lindsay. Paris: La Documentation Française, 1966. 987p.

A translation of *Les Institutions sociales de la France*. Designed to present a comprehensive picture of French social welfare institutions, 'it is purely descriptive and endeavours to be as concrete as possible'. Among the topics covered are social assistance, social security, public health, family policy, child welfare, juvenile delinquency, working conditions, and aid for the handicapped.

218 **The French Foreign Legion.**
James H. Wellard. Boston, Massachusetts: Little, Brown, 1974. 142p. bibliog.

This is a popular account of the *Légion etrangère*, based on research in the Legion's archives and on personal interviews with present and former legionnaires. The author describes his book as 'an attempt to study the Foreign Legion in the light of the integral role it has played in the history of the French Empire, in a reasonably objective manner, without romanticizing or abusing it'. The first chapter discusses the mystique of the unit; following chapters trace the Legion's history from 1831 to today. The volume is colourfully illustrated.

219 **French Foreign Legion.**
John Laffin. London: Dent, 1974. 179p. bibliog.

Laffin is a prolific writer of books on war and military history. His account of the French Foreign Legion covers much of the same ground as Wellard's book (previous item), but is more sensational: his first five chapters discuss charisma, philosophy, discipline and punishment, sex, and *le cafard* in the Legion. At the end of the volume is a selection of Legion songs and poems in French or German versions with English translations, and a short glossary of Legion slang.

Social Class, Social Groups, and Social Change

220 **Migration in post-war Europe: geographical essays.**
Edited by John Salt, Hugh D. Clout. London, New York: Oxford University Press, 1976. 228p. maps. bibliog.

A collection of essays designed to fill the gap caused by an absence of up-to-date studies on the role long-distance migration has played in changing the population map of Europe over the past thirty years. Rural-urban migration, international migration, and international labour migration in France are discussed in the context of the European situation.

Education

221 **French tradition in education: Ramus to Mme. Necker de Saussure.**
H. C. Barnard. Cambridge, England: Cambridge University Press, 1922. Reprinted, 1970. 319p. maps. bibliog.

A competent treatment of an interesting period in the history of French education. Barnard is also the author of an equally well-done survey *Education and the French Revolution*.

222 **Education in France.**
G. A. Male. Washington, D.C.: U.S. Dept. of Health, Education, and Welfare, 1963. 205p. map. bibliog. (U.S. Office of Education Bulletin, 1963, no. 33).

A United States government publication detailing education in France as of 1962. Gives the general characteristics of the educational system and a history of French education since the 18th century, then covers all types of schooling available: nursery, kindergarten, elementary, secondary, vocational, university, and specialized.

223 **French education since Napoleon.**
Joseph N. Moody. Syracuse, New York: Syracuse University Press, 1978. 252p. bibliog.

The author states in his preface that one of the purposes of his book is 'to test [the hypothesis of Pierre Bourdien - that education reinforces rather than alters the prevailing social differences of status, wealth, and culture] and to explore the dialectic between revolutionary proposals and established institutions'. This volume is a welcome addition to the literature available on French education, in that it is up to date - it discusses the educational reforms of 1977 - and well documented.

Education

224 **Histoire de l'enseignement en France, 1800-1967.** (History of education in France, 1800-1967.)
Antoine Prost. Paris: Armand Colin, 1968. 528p. bibliog. (U/Histoire contemporaine).

It is unfortunate that this survey of education in 19th and 20th century France has not been translated into English, as it is often cited as the best available history of French education for the modern period.

225 **Education and society in modern France.**
W. R. Fraser. London: Routledge & Kegan Paul; New York: Humanities Press, 1963. 140p. bibliog. (International Library of Sociology and Social Reconstruction).

Plans for reform of the educational system in France have succeeded each other with dizzying rapidity since the Second World War, with everyone agreeing that the schools are in need of radical reshaping and few agreeing on how this should be accomplished. Much of this book is translated from original French documentary material pertaining to this situation and lets the protagonists in the controversy speak for themselves. Administrative, professional, cultural, religious, and political obstacles to reform are fully discussed.

226 **Tomorrow's education: the French experience.**
J. Cappelle, translated from the French by W. D. Halls. Oxford, England; New York: Pergamon Press, 1967. 236p. (Commonwealth and International Library. Education and Educational Research Division).

Tomorrow's education means the democratization of French education. The author discusses why this change is necessary and how it should be done. The book includes basic data on the forms education has taken in France.

227 **Educational policy and planning: France.**
Paris: Organization for Economic Co-operation and Development, 1972. 695p.

Extensive changes have taken place in the French educational system in the last ten years. This volume was prepared by the OECD secretariat and French educational authorities as an aid in developing coherent policy and planning new programmes. It conveniently assembles detailed quantitative and qualitative information on education in France.

228 **Education, culture and politics in modern France.**
W. D. Halls. Oxford, England; New York: Pergamon Press, 1976. 2nd ed. 180p. bibliog.

An up-to-date presentation of the state of French education in the Fifth Republic, this work links French educational theory and practice with culture and politics during a particularly stressful time. The author covers the historical background of the educational system and the structure of school administration, relates the schools and teachers to society and discusses the politics of education. The section of the book that deals with the May 1968 student revolt and the subsequent reform of higher education is informative.

Education

229 **Classification of educational systems in OECD member countries: France, Norway, Spain.**
Paris: Organization for Economic Co-operation and Development, 1972. 134p. bibliog.

A book compiled as part of a project to facilitate comparison of educational systems in OECD member countries, this work emerges as a handy summary of the organization of the French school system. The sixty pages of the book devoted to France give useful information on pre-primary, primary, secondary, teacher, technical, university, and professional education. Length of study, entrance requirements, and other detailed items of information appear for each type of French educational institution. Foreigners will find this work helpful in understanding what French certificates certify - for example, the differences between the several doctorates granted by French universities.

230 **Higher education in France, 1848-1940.**
Theodore Zeldin. *Journal of Contemporary History*, vol. 2, pt. 3 (July 1967), p. 77-8.

In a special issue of the *Journal of Contemporary History* on the theme 'Education and social structure', the noted social historian Theodore Zeldin gives a brief history of higher education in France, centring on the oligarchical character of the universities and how they managed to preserve their privileged position in French society.

231 **European perspectives in teacher education.**
Edited by D. E. Lomax. New York: Wiley, 1976. 290p. bibliog.

Included in this collection of articles is B. Schwartz's 'A French model for teacher education', an essay which discusses proposals for innovations in the training of French upper secondary school teachers initiated by the government in 1969. Schwartz explores the role of the secondary school in French society, the constraints placed upon the project changes, and the reasons why the changes were never put into effect.

232 **The Sorbonne.**
J. G. Weightman. *Encounter*, vol. 16, pt. 6 (June 1961), p. 28-42.

Although this article was written before the events of 1968 initiated major changes in the French university system, it is still valuable for its perceptions of the problems inherent in the goals that French higher education sets for itself. The author contrasts the intellectual ambiance of the Sorbonne with that of its English counterparts, and explains the hurdles of the French competitive examination system that so affects student life.

233 **Sources of student protest in France.**
Raymond Boudon. *Annals of the American Academy of Political Science*, vol. 395 (May 1971), p. 139-49.

This interpretative essay on the French student crisis of 1968 has been reprinted in Philip G. Altbach and Robert S. Lauter's *The new pilgrim: youth protest in transition* (New York, 1972).

Education

234 **The French student uprising, November 1967-June 1968: an analytical record.**
Compiled by Alain Schnapp, Pierre Vidal-Naquet, translated from the French by Maria Jolas. Boston, Massachusetts: Beacon Press, 1971. 654p. bibliog.

A useful collection of basic documents on the French student rebellion of 1968. The editors provide a forty-eight page introductory chapter, 'Outline of a revolution', that is helpful in providing a perspective on the events. The volume also contains an extensive annotated bibliography on contemporary student issues.

Nationalities and Minorities

235 **La France des minorités.** (The France of the minorities.)
Paul Serant. Paris: Robert Laffont, 1965. 412p. maps. bibliog.

A very good survey of the non-French ethnic groups who live under the French government: Flemish, Bretons, Basques, *Languedociens* and Catalans, Corsicans, Alsatians, and *Lorrains*. Serant discusses their histories, languages, and traditions, as well as the organizations that promote their cultural and political aspirations. A final chapter considers the future of ethnic minorities in France and in Europe. The foreign reader will find the maps of the countries of these peoples particularly helpful.

236 **La France étrangère.** (Foreign France.)
Banine (pseud.) Paris: Desclée De Brouwer [n.d.]. 297p. (Editions SOS).

This book was written to alert the French public to the unfortunate situation in which many of those who have emigrated to France for political or economic reasons find themselves. An introductory chapter discusses relations between the French and emigrant groups in general, then separate chapters deal with specific groups and their problems. Algerians, Blacks, Portuguese, Yugoslavs, Spanish, and Russians are discussed. The final chapter depicts the *bidonvilles* where many emigrants live.

Nationalities and Minorities

237 **The limits of integration: ethnicity and nationalism in modern Europe.**
Edited by Oriol Pi-Sunyer. Amherst, Massachusetts: University of Massachusetts, Dept. of Anthropology, 1971. 187p. bibliog. (University of Massachusetts, Amherst. Dept. of Anthropology. Research Reports, no. 9, Oct. 1971).

This volume, which 'addresses itself to [the study of] interethnic relations in modern pluralistic societies', contains two essays on nationalistic movements among French ethnic groups. David H. Fortier's 'Breton nationalism and modern France: the permanent revolution' amounts to a capsule history of modern Breton nationalism; Fortier investigates 'the impact of techno-economic change on the genesis of nationalism', and 'the characteristic forms of nationalistic ideology, leadership and organization'. In William A. Douglass and Milton da Silva's 'Basque Nationalism', the French Basques in the department of the Basses Pyrénées are studied in the context of the much more critical Spanish situation. The authors conclude that 'the aspiration for a free Euzkadi or Basque nation carved out of Spain and France is a much greater challenge to Madrid than to Paris'.

238 **The roots of identity, three national movements in contemporary European politics.**
Patricia Elton Mayo. London: Allen Lane, 1970. 171p. maps. bibliog.

The author states that in this book she has 'attempted to examine a number of autonomous movements in Europe, not as isolated happenings but as symptoms of a basic imbalance in society'. Among the groups chosen for discussion are the Bretons and the Basques. Her book is noteworthy in that it devotes considerable space to the French Basques rather than centring attention, as is usual, on the Basques in Spain. Readers will find a good chapter on the economics of the French Basque provinces.

239 **Basques.**
Kenneth Medhurst. London: Minority Rights Group, 1972. 24p. bibliog. (Minority Rights Group, no. 9).

This short pamphlet by a British group concentrates on the Spanish Basque nationalist movement, but includes a few paragraphs on the 200,000 Basques who live on the French side of the Pyrenees and upon whom, according to this report, the Basque nationalist movement has had little impact.

240 **The Bretons against France: ethnic minority nationalism in twentieth-century Brittany.**
Jack E. Reece. Chapel Hill, North Carolina: University of North Carolina Press, 1977. 263p. maps. bibliog.

The author states in his preface that his study of 'ethnic minority nationalism in twentieth-century Brittany is intended to contribute to an understanding of the conditions under which an ethnic minority comes to advance political demands for self-government'. The Breton nationalist movement is studied in depth: its development, organization, leadership, policies, theories, relations with the French government, and perspectives for the future are fully covered.

Nationalities and Minorities

241 **The Alsatians.**
F. R. Alleman. *Encounter*, vol. 23, pt. 5 (Nov. 1964), p. 45-54.

The author of this excellent article comments that the problem of France's Alsatian minority is 'well-nigh unique...precisely [in the] fact that, in spite of their linguistic differences, the great majority of Alsatians regard themselves as entirely French'. Alleman outlines the history of Alsace, then discusses the Alsatian educational, linguistic, and economic situation in the 1960s. He also summarizes the policy of the French government towards this 'indisputably German people, culturally committed to France'.

242 **Regional identity and political change: the case of Alsace from the Third to the Fifth Republic.**
Malcolm Anderson. *Political Studies*, vol. 20, pt. 1 (March 1972), p. 17-30.

Analyses Alsace as an example of the problem of national identity and national allegiance in recent history. Concludes that 'the Alsatian case is of general interest because it emphasizes the difficulties and perhaps even the impossibility of characterizing a collective identity over a long period of time. In a timescale as short as the last sixty years it is difficult to describe the Alsatian identity as anything more than a gradually evolving linguistic tradition and an associated religious practice, on which feelings of distinctness have been anchored'.

243 **Voluntary associations among Ukrainians in France.**
Robert Anderson, Gallatin Anderson. *Anthropological Quarterly*, vol. 35, pt. 4 (Oct. 1962), p. 158-68.

Although the authors' purpose in this study is to examine the role voluntary associations play in the process of urbanization, readers will find this article informative on the general conditions and social relations of the minority Slavic ethnic group, the Ukrainian emigration to France, the acculturation and assimilation of the Ukrainians into French society, and the changing nature of the bonds that hold the Ukrainian community together.

244 **The North African in France: a French racial problem.**
David S. McLellan. *Yale Review*, vol. 44, pt. 3 (March 1955), p. 421-38.

This article, written while Algeria was still part of France, is a sobering presentation of the plight of the racially different Algerian worker in metropolitan France, where, in spite of his French citizenship, he was exploited by his employer, subject to social discrimination, and made the centre of unreasoning racial tensions and the target of police repression.

245 **The modernization of North African families in the Paris area.**
André Michel. The Hague: Mouton, 1972. 387p. bibliog.
(New Babylon: Studies in the Social Sciences, 16).

This sociological study on interethnic relations presents the results of research conducted in 1966-67 on the 'acculturation of Algerian immigrants in France in relation to French values and norms relative to the nuclear family'. It considers how 'modern' Algerian workers and their wives have become in their attitudes

Nationalities and Minorities

towards family size, contraception, and education. Nine hundred and fifty North African men and women living in the Paris area were interviewed for this study.

246 The North African immigrant in France.
Bernard Mounier, Jacques Dubuis. *International Journal of Mental Health*, vol. 5, pt. 2 (Summer 1976), p. 96-102.

A too-brief article that sketches the psychological problems faced by North Africans in metropolitan France. Discusses the emigrants' reasons for departure and the conditions necessary for their adjustment to French society.

247 Aspects of French Jewry: studies.
Georges Benguigui, Josiane Bijaoui-Rosenfeld, George Levitte. London: Valentine, Mitchell & Co., 1969. 142p. maps.

France has the largest Jewish population of any European country. But contemporary French Jewry is quite different from its pre-Second World War counterpart: 'At least fifty percent of the Jews [in France] today are recent arrivals from North Africa and the Middle East, with a culture and traditions entirely different from the French community of the past'. The three essays in this volume seek to present the 'present realities of Jewish community life', by focusing on the changes that have taken place within the Jewish community and on the factors associated with the assimilation and integration of new immigrants.

248 French citizenship and Jewish identity: a discussion.
Midstream, vol. 14, pt. 7 (Aug.-Sept.1968), p. 44-60.

A sharp crisis of identity occurred for French Jews in the autumn of 1967 as a result of the Six-Day War and President De Gaulle's remarks about Israel and the Jews at his press conference in November. This article is a transcription of a discussion held by the editors of the liberal Catholic periodical *Esprit* with four Jewish French intellectuals on the psychological and political implications of these two events for those who are both Jews and Frenchmen.

249 Anti-Semitism in modern France.
Robert F. Byrnes. New Brunswick, New Jersey: Rutgers University Press, 1950. 348p. bibliog. Reprinted, New York: Fertig, 1969.

This is the first volume of a projected two-volume case study of anti-Semitism in France, viewed as one aspect of a 19th century antidemocratic movement. The author has organized his material around the Dreyfus affair: this volume, entitled 'The prologue to the Dreyfus affair', describes 'the causes and course of the anti-Semitic movement in France before the explosion of the Dreyfus affair...[and] is therefore a history of France in Europe from the establishment of the Third Republic through 1894, with special emphasis upon the campaigns led against the Jews in France during those years'. The second volume of the work, which was never published, was to have covered the Dreyfus affair.

Statistics

250 **Annuaire statistique de la France.** (Statistical yearbook of France.)
Paris: Institut National de la Statistique et des Études Économiques, 1878-, annual.

The major statistical source for France, compiled under the direction of the Institut National de la Statistique et des Études Économiques, the central governmental organization for economic information. The main sections of the *Annuaire* are: geography and climate, population, economic resources (including agriculture, forestry, fisheries, and industry), transport, communications, internal trade, prices, incomes, consumption, finance, overall economic figures, and international data. The INSEE has also, since 1950, published a monthly bulletin of statistics, *Bulletin mensuel de statistique*, and, at irregular intervals, publishes an abridged version of the *Annuaire*.

251 **Publications statistiques des administrations.** (Statistical publications of the administrations.)
Institut National de la Statistique et des Études Économiques. Paris: Observatoire Économique de Paris, 1974. 75p.

An extremely useful bibliography that lists all the statistical publications issued by departments of the French government.

252 **Principaux résultats du recensement de 1975.** (Principal results of the census of 1975.)
Paris: Institut National de la Statistique et des Études Économiques, 1977. 210p. (INSEE, 238; Démographie et Emploi, 52).

French demographers conduct a general census every ten years, in the fifth year of the decade. This publication is a handy summary of census data collected in the 1975 census.

Statistics

253 **European historical statistics, 1750-1970.**
B. R. Mitchell. New York: Columbia University Press, 1975. 827p.

An authoritative compendium of numerical data that includes statistics for France, taken from the *Annuaire statistique de la France* (q.v.), for the years 1878 to 1970. Researchers will find data on France's climate, population, labour force, agriculture, industry, external trade, transport, communications, finance, prices, education, and national accounts.

254 **The female population of France in the nineteenth century: a reconstruction of 82 departments.**
Etienne Van De Walle. Princeton, New Jersey: Princeton University Press, 1974. 483p. bibliog.

This is a compilation of statistical tables, assembled in order 'to present the statistical basis of a proposed analysis of the social and economic factors responsible for the decline of fertility in nineteenth-century France'.

Politics

255 **The French political system.**
Maurice Duverger, translated from the French by Barbara North, Robert North. Chicago, Illinois: University of Chicago Press, 1958. 227p. (Chicago Library of Comparative Politics).

This often-cited book is a good place to take one's bearings in regard to the French political system as it existed under the Fourth Republic. The work is organized in three parts: government institutions, political forces, and individual liberty, with the last section including a very interesting discussion of civil rights in France. The text of the constitution of the Fourth Republic is included in an appendix.

256 **Patterns of government: the major political systems of Europe.**
Edited by Samuel H. Beer, Adam B. Ulam. New York: Random House, 1973. 3rd ed. 778p. bibliog.

This standard work on European politics contains a chapter entitled 'The French political system' by Suzanne Berger that is an excellent summary of the structure of contemporary French politics. Berger begins by discussing the 'tradition of modernity', then surveys the factors that contribute to the nation's politics: political legitimacy and the constitutional order; the development of the party system in France; the changing politics of policy-making; and local government in a strongly centralized state.

257 **Politics in France.**
Pierre Avril, translated from the French by John Ross. Harmondsworth, England: Penguin Books, 1969. 304p. bibliog. (Pelican Books).

A deft summary of the 'French style of government' by a French journalist who is a keen observer of the political scene. Avril examines the roles prescribed for presidents, ministers, civil servants, members of parliament, and political leaders under the successive French republics, concluding that French politics pivots on a search for an elusive balance between authority and democracy.

Politics

258 French electoral systems and elections since 1789.
Peter Campbell. Hamden, Connecticut: Archon, 1958.
Reprinted, 1965. 155p. bibliog.

As the author notes in his preface, electoral systems have changed continually in France since 1789, more often than not being regarded as a weapon wielded by a political or social group in its struggle for control of the state rather than as a neutral technique for the selection of public officials. The author provides a detailed study of the part played by electoral systems in French politics from 1789 to 1962. His explanation of the phenomenon - what the systems were and how they worked - will undoubtedly remain the basic account for years to come.

259 Political parties and elections in the French Fifth Republic.
J. R. Frears. New York: St. Martin's Press, 1977. 292p. bibliog.

An up-to-date, well-written account of contemporary French political parties that should clarify the scene for the general reader and provide a starting point for the student of contemporary French politics. After an introductory overview of the current French situation when, as the author comments, 'it appears possible...to affirm that for the first time since the eighteenth century no social group challenges the institutions of the Republic', chapters are devoted to all the active political parties: Gaullists, *Giscardiens*, centrists, socialists and left-wing radicals, communists, and fringe parties of the Left and the Right. Electoral behaviour is discussed, and detailed information on the issues and results of the Fifth Republic's elections - presidential, parliamentary, local, and national referenda - is provided.

260 The French polity.
William Safran. New York: McKay, 1977. 332p. bibliog.

An up-to-date textbook on the political organization of France. The author details the structure and institutions of the French government, discussing their development and how political forces interact in the French multiparty state.

261 France and the West: concerns and hopes.
Jean-Baptiste Duroselle. *Review of Politics*, vol. 39, pt. 4 (Oct. 1977), p. 451-72.

An article by an eminent French political scientist on the political situation in France prior to the 1978 spring elections. Of most interest is Duroselle's analysis of the strength of the French Left and its prospects for success in the elections.

262 Politics and society in contemporary France.
Comparative Politics, vol. 10, pt. 1 (Oct. 1977), p. 1-179.

This special issue of *Comparative Politics* is edited by Ezra N. Suleiman. The articles that compose the issue were written at a time when the Left was considered to be close to receiving an electoral mandate in the 1978 elections, a result that would perhaps have signalled the end of the Fifth Republic. The essays, however, focus on problems of French politics and society that are complex and deep-seated, and that would require more than a shift in electoral support from the Right to the Left to solve. Contents: 'The Right in France since 1945' (Francois Bourricaud); 'The French Left under the Fifth Republic: the search for identity in unity' (Howard Machin and Vincent Wright); 'The reform of local government: a political analysis' (Peter Gourevitch); 'The French univer-

Politics

sity since 1968' (Raymond Boudon); 'D'une boutique a l'autre: changes in the organization of the traditional middle classes from the Fourth to Fifth Republic' (Suzanne Berger); 'The myth of technical expertise: selection, organization, and leadership' (Ezra N. Suleiman); 'Religion, class, and politics' (Guy Michelat and Michel Simon).

263 Crisis and compromise: politics in the Fourth Republic.
Philip M. Williams. Hamden, Connecticut: Archon, 1964. 3rd ed. 546p. bibliog.

The best work available on the workings of the French parliamentary system of the Fourth Republic. Indispensable reading for those who wish to understand how the political parties of the Fourth Republic interacted.

264 Affluence and the French worker in the Fourth Republic.
Richard F. Hamilton. Princeton, New Jersey: Princeton University Press, 1967. 323p. map. bibliog.

'This is a study of French working-class politics. Its primary concern is to locate the social structural roots of political attitudes and voting behavior.' A very interesting volume, that contains much pertinent information on the French worker, his social position and his psychology.

265 French army in politics, 1945-1962.
John S. Ambler. Columbus, Ohio: Ohio State University Press, 1966. 427p. bibliog.

A good study of the relation of the French military establishment to civilian politics. The author states in his preface that his analysis will focus on the problem of civilian control of the French army, and that 'French military politics will be examined primarily from the standpoint of threats to the civilian political régime'.

Political Parties, Groups, and Movements

266 The right wing in France: from 1815 to De Gaulle.
René Remond, translated from the French by J. M. Laux. Philadelphia, Pennsylvania: University of Pennsylvania Press, 1969. 2nd American ed. 465p. bibliog.

Discounting the idea that the French Right can be 'reduced to the unity of one tradition and one way of thinking', Rémond studies the rightist groups of France from the Ultras of 1815 to those of the Fifth Republic. His book is intended to fill a gap in studies of the Right by presenting systematically the different tendencies of those groups and movements that can be classified as politically conservative. The reader will find information on Orleanism, Legitimism, Bonapartism, Boulangism, *Action Française, Bloc National*, Poujadism, fascism, and other rightist movements.

267 Conservative politics in France.
Malcolm Anderson. London: Allen & Unwin, 1974. 381p. bibliog.

A study of right-wing parties in France, specifically designed to complement Rémond's account of right-wing attitudes and tendencies (previous item). Anderson's book begins in 1880 and extends into the post-De Gaulle era.

268 *Action Française*: royalism and reaction in twentieth-century France.
Eugen Weber. Stanford, California: Stanford University Press, 1962. 594p. bibliog.

This is a scholarly treatment of the *Action Française* by a well-known historian, and can be regarded as the definitive monograph on the subject. Covers the

Political Parties, Groups, and Movements

history of the movement from its beginning in 1899 to its end after the Second World War.

269 **The *Action Française*: die-hard reactionaries in twentieth-century France.**
Edward R. Tannenbaum. New York: Wiley, 1962. 316p. bibliog.

A book best read in conjunction with Weber's monograph on the rightist organization (previous item). Tannenbaum analyses the intellectual basis for the ideology of the supporters of the *Action Française*.

270 **Three faces of fascism.**
Ernst Nolte, translated from the German by Leila Vennewitz. New York: Holt, Rinehart & Winston, 1966. 561p. bibliog.

In the second part of this book, the author discusses Charles Maurras and the *Action Française*. His analysis of the movement - its doctrine, history, development, practices, and style - is thorough and penetrating. The reader will find it illuminating to view the *Action Française* in the context of the fascistic movements of 1919-45 Europe - Italian Fascism and German National Socialism.

271 **Gaullism: the rise and fall of a political movement.**
Anthony Hartley. New York: Outerbridge & Dienstfrey, 1971. 373p. bibliog.

A perceptive analysis of a phenomenon that the author feels 'is not only the result of the impact of a single man on the course of French history...[but] at once a political movement and a political doctrine'. The book traces Gaullism from its rise in 1940, through its zenith of power 1958-69, to its decline with the resignation of De Gaulle in 1969, studying it in relation to the Fourth Republic, the Algerian War, and the foreign and domestic policy of the Fifth Republic. An excellent bibliographical essay evaluates the pertinent literature for those who wish to pursue the subject.

272 **The founding of the French Socialist Party, 1893-1905.**
Aaron Noland. Cambridge, Massachusetts: Harvard University Press, 1956. 233p. bibliog. Reprinted, New York: Fertig, 1970.

The founding of the French Socialist party (*Parti Socialiste, Section Française de l'Internationale Ouvrière*) in 1905 was the result of the merging of several socialist parties and factions during the 1893-1905 period. Noland's history of this development is considered the standard account.

273 **The communist parties of Italy and France: a study in comparative communism.**
Thomas H. Greene. *World Politics*, vol. 21, pt. 1 (Oct. 1968), p. 1-38.

An astute anlysis of two nonruling communist parties that is useful in clarifying the differences between them and the part each plays in a multiparty system.

Political Parties, Groups, and Movements

274 **French communism, 1920-1972.**
Ronald Tiersky. New York: Columbia University Press, 1974. 425p. bibliog.

A scholarly study, one of the first to appear in English, this book is very likely to remain the basic history of the party for the period covered for some time to come. The first section of the volume is a political history of French communism; the second part is an analysis of the phenomenon of French communism in itself and in relation to French politics and society. One of the most interesting parts of the book is Tiersky's analysis of the 'four dominant roles the [communist] movement plays in French life': its two hardline classic roles of revolutionary vanguard and countercommunity, and its two collaborative moderate roles of popular tribune and government party. The annotated bibliography should be very helpful to students.

275 **French communism in the making, 1914-1924.**
Robert Wohl. Stanford, California: Stanford University Press, 1966. 530p. bibliog.

A detailed history of the pre-Bolshevist French Communist Party. Another excellent history of the party is Daniel R. Brouwer's *New Jacobins; the French Communist Party and the Popular Front, 1934-1938* (Ithaca, New York: Cornell University Press, 1968).

276 **Communism and the French intellectuals, 1914-1960.**
David Caute. New York: Macmillan, 1964. 412p. bibliog.

A thorough study of the relationship between French intellectuals and the French Communist Party from 1914 to 1960. The author analyses the contradictions between intellectual values and membership in an authoritarian organization, concluding that the fate of those who remained in the party was 'tragic' as their intellectual development was stifled. Especially interesting is Caute's discussion of the involvements of André Gide, André Malraux, and Jean-Paul Sartre with the party.

277 **The French communists: profile of a people.**
Annie Kriegel, translated from the French by Elaine P. Halperin. Chicago, Illinois: University of Chicago Press, 1972. 408p. bibliog.

The author describes a half-century of French communism from an ethnographical perspective, focusing on the French Communist Party as 'a minority Bolshevik society which exists within the confines of a liberal polity'. Her viewpoint illuminates the paradox of the conservatism of this revolutionary group. Moving from the outer to the inner circles of party membership, the author provides insights into the psychological aspects of communist commitment, including a very interesting sketch of Maurice Thorez. Her bibliographical note on the historiography of French communism is an excellent evaluation of sources and available literature.

278 **Communism in Italy and France.**
Edited by D. L. M. Blackmer, Sidney Tarrow. Princeton, New Jersey: Princeton University Press, 1975. 651p. bibliog.

The editors have gathered together fifteen essays by fourteen political scientists comparing the *Parti Communiste Français* with the *Partito Communista Italiano*.

Political Parties, Groups, and Movements

The result is revealing of the assumptions upon which the French party operates and the place it occupies in French society. In many ways, its selective, élitist, doctrinaire orientation is in direct contrast to the Italian communists' position. Tarrow's concluding essay considers prospects for change as the French communists' pro-Soviet posture becomes less tenable in the context of world politics.

279 **The French Communist Party in transition: PCF-CPSU relations and the challenge to Soviet authority.**
Annette E. Stiefbold. New York: Praeger, 1977. 155p. bibliog. (Praeger Special Studies in International Politics and Government).

Stiefbold studies the *Parti Communiste Français* from 1968 to 1977, viewing the period as one during which the PCF, shaken by the events of May-June 1968, gradually asserted its autonomy from the Soviet Communist Party (CPSU), reevaluated itself, and moved closer to the Eurocommunist position held by its sister parties in Spain and Italy. Current French Communist Party policy plays down the ideology of proletarian internationalism and downgrades the Soviet claim to leadership in the communist world.

280 **The French communists and the Union of the Left, 1974-1976.**
Ian Campbell. *Parliamentary Affairs*, vol. 29, pt. 3 (Summer 1976), p. 246-63.

An interesting article discussing relations between leftist parties in France, written at the time when it seemed possible that the communists would participate in the government after the 1978 elections. The author discusses 'the debate among French communists as to their objectives and the means by which they can be most effectively secured'.

281 **The French democratic Left, 1963-1969: toward a modern party system.**
Frank L. Wilson. Stanford, California: Stanford University Press, 1971. 258p. bibliog.

The author manages to clarify the politics of the non-communist French Left during the six final years of the De Gaulle régime.

Foreign Relations

282 **The foreign policy of France from 1914 to 1945.**
J. Nere. London: Routledge & Kegan Paul, 1975. 376p. bibliog. (Foreign Policies of the Great Powers series).

Firsthand documentation of the diplomatic events of 1914-45 is a problem for the historian: the archives of the French Ministry of Foreign Affairs were destroyed or scattered in May 1940; thus, the entire diplomatic history of the period may never be written. This, then, is an important book: Nere has made use of the sources available, and has achieved his aim of providing the reader with 'a general understanding of French policy reduced to its outstanding features'. His excellent bibliography evaluates and discusses his sources.

283 **French foreign policy since the Second World War.**
Herbert Tint. London: Weidenfeld & Nicolson, 1972. 273p. (Foreign Policy Studies).

A good presentation of the policies followed by France after the Second World War. Studies the new relationship with West Germany and French attempts to balance the Soviets against the Americans. Includes some very interesting sections on the less-than-successful French efforts to build relations with Third World nations through economic, technological, and cultural ties. A chapter on the organization of the French diplomatic service is a helpful introduction to the departments of the Quai D'Orsay.

284 **French foreign policy under De Gaulle.**
Alfred Grosser, translated from the French by L. A. Pattison. Boston, Massachusetts: Little, Brown, 1967. 175p. bibliog.

This book is a revision of Grosser's *La Politique extérieure de la Cinquième République*, with a chapter, 'And now...' added especially for the English edition. It is an analysis of Fifth Republic foreign policy that centres on the personal style of De Gaulle's leadership as it expressed itself in a foreign policy that dared to take risks.

Foreign Relations

285 De Gaulle and the world: the foreign policy of the Fifth French Republic.
W. W. Kulski. Syracuse, New York: Syracuse University Press, 1966. 428p. bibliog.

A large volume that touches upon all aspects of French foreign policy from 1958 to 1965, emphasizing De Gaulle's role in its formulation. Includes a perceptive analysis of De Gaulle in his role of 'charismatic leader'.

286 French international policy under De Gaulle and Pompidou: the politics of grandeur.
Edward A. Kolodziej. Ithaca, New York: Cornell University Press, 1974. 618p. bibliog.

A massive volume examining key points of French global policy under the Fifth Republic's first two régimes, 1958 to 1974, a time when the French attempted to change the 'alignment patterns and the distribution of power among states'. The author writes informatively of French relations with other Western European countries, with North Africa, and with Middle Eastern nations. There is also a good section on France with and without NATO.

287 Foreign policy and interdependence in Gaullist France.
Edward L. Morse. Princeton, New Jersey: Princeton University Press, 1973. 336p. bibliog.

An attempt to reconcile the particular experience of French foreign policy with a general explanation of contemporary foreign policy. The first part of the book presents the author's theoretical framework; the second part is a detailed case study of French foreign policy during De Gaulle's presidency. According to Morse, 'what has made French foreign policy in the 1960s so fascinating is the way a generalized condition of contemporary foreign policy was brought into sharp focus by the fact that the president of Fifth Republic France was so blatantly anachronistic'.

288 De Gaulle and the Anglo-Saxons.
John Newhouse. New York: Viking Press, 1970. 371p. bibliog.

A readable presentation of the relations between France, the United States, and Great Britain during a period beginning shortly before De Gaulle's return to power and ending with his resignation as president and withdrawal from politics in 1969. The diplomacy of these years was troubled and complex: Algeria, the Berlin crisis, the Common Market, NATO, nuclear policy, and Southeast Asia, all afforded rich opportunities for misunderstandings and strain between De Gaulle and his Anglo-Saxon allies. Much of the book draws upon information obtained in private conversations for, as Newhouse comments in his preface, many of the official documents of this period will not be available for some time to come.

Foreign Relations

289 France and the United States: from the beginnings to the present day.
Jean-Baptiste Duroselle, translated from the French by Derek Coltman. Chicago, Illinois: University of Chicago Press, 1978. 280p. bibliog. (U.S. and the World: Foreign Perspectives series).

An eminent French diplomatic historian traces the entire course of Franco-American relations. France's influence was strong during the early period of United States history following the American Revolutionary War, but weakened in the 19th century. Close contact revived with the First World War and has continued through to the present. Duroselle concentrates his analysis on the post-1914 period, studying psychological and intellectual aspects of Franco-American relations, as well as political and diplomatic.

290 America and French culture, 1750-1848.
Howard Mumford Jones. Chapel Hill, North Carolina: University of North Carolina Press; London: Oxford University Press, 1927. 615p. bibliog.

This older work was a pioneer effort, the first to try, in the author's words, 'to put the pieces together', and 'to see the general American attitude to things French'. The chronological boundaries of the study were chosen as bracketing the period of most intense French interaction with the new American culture. The author traces the Franco-American cultural relationship in connection with America's maturing concept of herself, covering the French migration to the United States, the French language and French manners in America, and the influence of French religious, philosophical and educational ideas on the new country.

291 American and French culture, 1800-1900: interchanges in art, science, literature and society.
Henry Blumenthal. Baton Rouge, Louisiana: Louisiana State University Press, 1975. 554p. bibliog.

An account of the cross-fertilization that occurred in the 19th century when, in the author's words, 'bourgeois France met Puritan America'. All areas of interaction are discussed: philosophy, literature, theatre, music and dance, painting, sculpture, architecture, natural sciences, dentistry, and medicine. The book is solid and factual; its bibliography is forty-seven pages long.

292 France and the European Community.
Edited by Sydney Nettleton Fisher. Columbus, Ohio: Ohio State University Press, 1964. 176p. bibliog.

A revised and expanded version of papers presented by eight contributors at a conference held at the Graduate Institute for World Affairs of Ohio State University in October 1963. It is basically a state-of-the-art report on France in relation to the then six-year-old European Community, a report coloured by the shock of De Gaulle's rejection on 14 January 1963 of Britain's entry into the organization. Titles of the papers: 'French culture and the European Community: the complexity of survival'; 'The legal structure of the European Community'; 'France and European security'; 'French politicians and the European Communities: the record of the 1950s'; 'Agriculture in France and the European Community'; 'European economic integration in a new phase'; 'France and the resource

Foreign Relations

pattern of Western Europe'; 'The Soviet bloc, the Common Market, and France'. The last essay, relating France to Eastern Europe, is written by Zbigniew Brzezinski.

293 The general says no.
Nora Beloff. Harmondsworth, England: Penguin Books, 1963. 180p.

A journalistic account of De Gaulle's veto on 14 January 1963 of Britain's bid for membership in the European Economic Community.

294 Collision in Brussels: the Common Market crisis of 30 June 1965.
John Newhouse. New York: W. W. Norton, 1967. 195p. bibliog. (Toqueville series).

'The crisis of 30 June was an example par excellence of de Gaulle's technique, with every weapon in play. It was also the first real test of the Common Market, and sheds some, if not much, light on the Community's method as well as its character and prospects. Finally and perhaps most important, it was a political test of strength between European states'.

295 A tacit alliance: France and Israel from Suez to the Six-Day War.
Sylvia K. Crosbie. Princeton, New Jersey: Princeton University Press, 1974. 280p. bibliog. (Modern Middle East series, 7).

From 1956 to 1967, France and Israel formed a defence and military alliance that differed from patterns of alignment normally practised in international politics. This book analyses the unconventional relationship as it arose, evolved, and finally ended, placing it 'within the framework of the complex and often confusing interplay of the international, regional, and domestic [political] systems'.

296 The French presence in Black Africa.
Edward M. Corbett. Washington, D.C.: Black Orpheus Press, 1972. 209p. bibliog.

'This study undertakes an analysis of sufficient detail to provide the basis for an appreciation of the sociocultural, political, military, and economic processes through which France exerts predominant influence in the new republics south of the Sahara. Its aim is to delineate the essential elements of France's current position there and to envision its probable evolution.' The book covers the fourteen nations that were formerly the French territories of West and Equatorial Africa and Madagascar.

297 Atomic energy policy in France under the Fourth Republic.
Laurence Scheineman. Princeton, New Jersey: Princeton University Press, 1965. 259p. bibliog.

A volume that is revealing of the internal political process which led to the first French-sponsored nuclear explosion at Reggane on 13 February 1960, and France's début as a nuclear power. The first section of the book covers the development of nuclear policy during the years 1946-51, detailing the background

Foreign Relations

and structure of the *Commissariat à l'Energie Atomique (CEA)*; the second section traces the history of the *force de frappe* to the Fifth Republic.

298 **French nuclear diplomacy.**
Wilfred L. Kohl. Princeton, New Jersey: Princeton University Press, 1971. 412p. bibliog.

The idea of a French nuclear strike force did not originate with the president of the Fifth Republic; nevertheless, France's 'nuclear force was intrinsically related to [De Gaulle's] political goals of ensuring France's independence and augmenting France's freedom of action in world affairs'. This book is a complete discussion of the *force de frappe* as the mainstay of De Gaulle's foreign policy - for the West as well as for the East.

299 **France defeats EDC.**
Edited by Daniel Lerner, Raymond Aron. New York: Praeger, 1957. 225p.

On 20th August 1954, France rejected the European Defence Community by a vote in the National Assembly. This book is a collection of essays by experts analysing the factors that led up to and the implications of that refusal. Covers the setting, the stakes, and the roles taken in the controversy by the press, the public, and the government.

300 **French foreign policy: the domestic debate.**
Marie-Claude Smouts. *International Affairs*, vol. 53, pt. 1 (Jan. 1977), p. 36-50.

A good summary of recent French foreign policy. According to the author, 'under the presidency of Valéry Giscard d'Estaing perceptible modifications in foreign policy have been introduced', but 'the internal debate on foreign policy is muffled', and 'a vague malaise surrounds diplomacy'.

301 **Europe from below: an assessment of Franco-German popular contacts.**
John E. Farquharson, Stephen C. Holt. New York: St. Martin's Press, 1975. 218p. bibliog.

The authors consider an aspect of foreign relations that has not received attention: the part played by popular contacts in international relations. The Franco-German *rapprochement* of recent years is particularly interesting in this regard and lends itself well to this study. The book covers national cultural policies, youth exchange programmes, academic exchange programmes, economic ties, relations between workers, the twinning of towns, and the role of private initiative in Franco-German understanding.

Government and Administration

302 **The government and politics of France.**
Dorothy Pickles. London: Methuen, 1972-73. 2 vols. bibliog.

A basic work by an expert on the politics and government of the Fifth Republic. These volumes supersede the author's *Fifth French Republic*, 3rd ed. (New York, 1966). The first volume covers the constitutional framework and the political institutions of contemporary France; the second volume analyses French politics since 1958, with a section on foreign policy. The book contains an English translation of the constitution of the Fifth Republic.

303 **France: government and society; an historical survey.**
Edited by J. M. Wallace-Hadrill, John McManners. London: Methuen, 1970. 2nd ed. 275p. bibliog.

A book that can be highly recommended. This is a collection of essays by historians and scholars that follows the history of the interaction between government and society in France from prehistoric Gaul down to the Fourth Republic. An excellent place to begin the study of French constitutional history. Well-selected bibliographies are appended to each essay.

304 **The government and politics of France.**
John S. Ambler, with Laurence Scheineman. Boston, Massachusetts: Houghton Mifflin, 1971. 257p. map. bibliog.

A lucid presentation and analysis of the workings of the French government under the Fifth Republic. Covers the French political tradition, society and politics, parties and elections, government institutions, the dual executive, parliament, the administration, and foreign policy. A perceptive chapter on legitimacy, governmental performance, and stability has practical reference to contemporary France. The appendix includes an abridged version of the constitution of 1958.

Government and Administration

305 The French parliament (1958-1967).
Philip M. Williams. London: Allen & Unwin, 1968. 136p. bibliog. (Studies in Political Science, 2).

A compact account, by a leading British political scientist, of how the French parliament functions within the framework imposed upon it by the constitution of 1958 and the political conditions of the French Republic. The author focuses his discussion on the years from 1962 to 1967, when the Gaullists were in the majority in the National Assembly, in order to give a picture of 'normal' parliamentary operations under the Fifth Republic.

306 Government in France: an introduction to the executive power.
Malcolm Anderson. New York; Oxford, England: Pergamon Press, 1970. 217p.

Under the Fifth Republic, political power and state authority are primarily exercised by the executive branch of the government. Students of this phenomenon will welcome this introductory survey for its clear presentation of the structure and function of the executive of the French central government. Covers the history and constitutional background of the executive, the presidency under the Fifth Republic, the functions of the prime minister and the government ministries, and the relationship between society and the executive.

307 The *Conseil d'État* in modern France.
Charles E. Freedman. New York: Columbia University Press, 1961. 205p. bibliog. (Columbia Studies in the Social Sciences, 603).

The *Conseil d'État* acts as legal advisor to the French government, providing it with interpretations of the constitution and the law. It also drafts legislation and has court functions. This book examines the workings of this institution, tracing its development from the fall of the Second Empire to the advent of the Fifth Republic, and inquiring into the nature and scope of the transformations that the *Conseil* has undergone during these years, in its internal structure, in its role vis-à-vis the government, and as France's highest administrative court.

308 The administrative functions of the French *Conseil d'État*.
Margherita Rendel. London: Weidenfeld & Nicolson, 1970. 320p. bibliog. (London School of Economics Monographs, 6).

The author states in her preface that there 'has been so far no work in any language, not even in French, which attempts to present within the covers of a single volume a complete picture of the administrative work of the *Conseil*'. Rendel's comprehensive presentation of the *Conseil's* administrative functions will remedy this situation. The book covers the history, membership, organization, methods of work, and supervisory operations of the institution, as well as its role in the interpretation of law and the drafting of legislation.

Government and Administration

309 **The French deputy: incentives and behavior in the National Assembly.**
Oliver H. Woshinsky. Lexington, Massachusetts: D. C. Heath, 1973. 232p. bibliog.

Woshinsky conducted more than fifty personal interviews with members of the 1969 National Assembly in order to find out what French politicians are really like. His study focuses on the motives and actions of the deputies, in particular on their incentives for entering politics. The reader of this book will learn whether the stereotype of the French politician as an ideologue or an opportunist has any basis in reality.

310 **The French budgetary process.**
Guy Lord. Berkeley, California: University of California Press, 1973. 217p. bibliog.

The author feels that the advent of the National Plan in France has not diminished the importance of the budget; he has written this book in order 'to describe the French budgetary process as it operates today, and how economic and financial decisions are made within the framework of that process'. In his view, the budget process illustrates decision making in the Fifth Republic, and he studies it from an administrative perspective, rather than as a legislative or accounting procedure. His approach to his material is nontechnical: after an historical overview of the development of financial procedures in France, 1789-1958, he discusses the constitutional framework for the budget and the activities and strategies utilized by the ministries and parliament in determining it. The 1967 budget is used as an example.

311 **French technocracy and comparative government.**
F. F. Ridley. *Political Studies*, vol. 14, pt. 1 (Feb. 1966), p. 34-52.

A perceptive treatment of the 'technocrats' in the French government and public administration. The author defines technocracy, elucidates the technocratic outlook, and discusses the implications for the state of the technocratic style of 'scientific management of society'. The article ends with an assessment of the pros and cons of the technocrat in government.

312 **Public administration in France.**
F. Ridley, J. Blondel. London: Routledge & Kegan Paul; New York: Barnes & Noble, 1969. 2nd ed. 391p. bibliog.

A book that has been rightly called 'the standard textbook for English-speaking students' in the field. Originally published in 1964, the second edition has an additional chapter on the reforms of 1965-67. The first part of the volume gives the framework of administration: the presidency and the government, the civil service, the government departments, and local government. The second part of the book explains the organization of public services: the administration of justice, the maintenance of public order, financial and economic administration, public enterprise, technical administration, education and cultural affairs, and welfare services. Peter Campbell has provided the book with an introduction, 'The state and society in France', that concisely summarizes the principles underlying the French administrative system.

Government and Administration

313 **The European administrative élite.**
John A. Armstrong. Princeton, New Jersey: Princeton University Press, 1973. 406p. bibliog.

A comparative study of the men in the top administrative positions in France, Germany, Great Britain, and the USSR. Examines their definitions of their roles, their socialization and recruitment into the élite, their value systems, and their educational and career patterns.

314 **Politics, power, and bureaucracy in France: the administrative élite.**
Ezra N. Suleiman. Princeton, New Jersey: Princeton University Press, 1974. 440p. bibliog.

A complete examination by a political scientist of the French civil service and the executive departments of the French government. Suleiman deftly threads his way through the corridors of power: he discusses the backgrounds of French administrators, their channels of recruitment, and their self-perceptions. The volume contains a very interesting section on the relations of top bureaucrats with politicians, and with the country at large.

315 **The mandarins of Western Europe: the political roles of top civil servants.**
Edited by Mattei Dogan. Beverly Hills, California: Sage Publications, 1975. 314p. bibliog.

The past decade has seen the appearance of several excellent studies on European government executives (including the two previous items). This collection of essays is another noteworthy contribution to the study of those in public service who occupy positions where administrative and political power coincide. Two essays on French administrators are included in this volume: 'French ministerial staffs', by Jeanne Siwek-Pouydesseau, and 'The managers of public enterprises in France', by Daniel Derivry.

316 **The French civil service.**
Roger Gregoire. Brussels: International Institute of Administrative Science, 1964. 363p.

This is a major source in English for information on an aspect of French governmental structure about which little is written even in French. The author summarizes the origin and evolution of the French notion of the civil service, then describes the civil service as of 1962: structure, organization of careers, training and selection of personnel, career progress and the rating system, remuneration of officials, and professional ethics.

317 **The prefects and provincial France.**
Brian Chapman. London: Allen & Unwin, 1955. 246p. bibliog.

A lucid, well-organized study of the prefectoral corps, a feature of the French government and administration difficult for a foreigner to grasp. Covers the history of the corps, its administrative functions, and the responsibilities of the *chef de cabinet* the sub-prefect and the prefect.

Government and Administration

318 **The parliament of France.**
D. W. S. Lidderdale. London: Hansard Society, 1951. 296p.

For those wishing to understand the workings - and the flaws - of the parliamentary system of the Fourth Republic. An expert description of the procedures, rules, and customs of the parliament of France during those turbulent years. The first two chapters of the book give an interesting account of the historical, constitutional, and political factors that shaped relations between the French parliament and the government.

319 **On the game of politics in France.**
Nathan C. Leites. Stanford, California: Stanford University Press, 1959. 190p.

A book that successfully communicates the style of the institutional life of the French parliament, delineating the 'major patterns of parliamentary strategy and tactics...in the Fourth Republic from 1951 to 1958'. Although not inaccurate, the work tends towards caricature. For a more objective account of the Fourth Republic's parliament, the reader can turn to Duncan MacRae Jr.'s *Parliament, parties, and society in France, 1946-1958* (New York: St. Martin's Press, 1967).

320 **The government of the French [Third] Republic.**
Walter R. Sharp. New York: Van Nostrand, 1938. 373p. bibliog.

This is the best source for the structure of the government of the Third Republic (1870-1940); it covers the leadership, parliament, administration, maintenance of order, economic *étatisme*, and the social welfare system of the régime. Last chapter 'French democracy faces a troubled world'.

321 **Introduction to French local government.**
Brian Chapman. London: Allen & Unwin, 1953. 238p. bibliog. Reprinted, Westport, Connecticut: Hyperion Press, 1979.

Although it is now over twenty-five years old, this book remains a fundamental source for information on the workings of local government in France. The volume is written particularly for the English reader: it begins with an overview of the areas subject to local administration and an introduction to the personnel of local government, underlining the differences between French and English administrative law as applied at the local level. Explanations are then given of the work of elected bodies and administrators, the relationship between administrative courts and local government, and the organization of local government finance. A separate chapter details the organization of Paris. Three helpful charts are provided: (1) the organization of a commune; (2) the organization of a prefecture; and (3) the organization of the Ministry of the Interior.

322 **The ambiguous consensus: a study of local government in France.**
Mark Kesselman. New York: Knopf, 1967. 201p. bibliog.

Between 1962 and 1964, Kesselman interviewed more than fifty French municipal government officials - mostly mayors - in the Calvados and the Gironde. His study of the 'grass-roots consensus' basic to French government is based upon

Government and Administration

these interviews. The book also includes a perceptive discussion of *apolitisme*: Kesselman's exploration of this concept and its implications is a valuable contribution to the study of French politics.

323 **Between center and periphery: grassroots politicians in Italy and France.**
Sidney Tarrow. New Haven, Connecticut: Yale University Press, 1977. 272p.

A recent and welcome addition to the small amount of material available in English on local government in France. This study centres on the role of the mayor in the crucial competition among outlying regions for resources under the control of the central government. A well-written presentation, based on firsthand research.

Law and Constitution

324 French law: its structure, sources and methodology.
René David, translated from the French by Michael Kindred. Baton Rouge, Louisiana: Louisiana State University Press, 1972. 222p.

A very informative volume, written specifically for those whose legal systems - in contrast to the French - are modelled on common law. Its purpose is to demonstrate the principles upon which French law is based, to describe how French lawyers reason, and to point out how French principles and ratiocination differ from those upon which common law is founded. Chapters describe the French legal tradition, the political, administrative and judicial organization of France, and the French concept of law. An appendix contains information on the teaching of law in France.

325 The *Code Napoléon* and the common-law world.
Edited by Bernard Schwartz. New York: New York University Press, 1956. 438p. bibliog.

The *Code Napoléon* - the French Civil Code - was voted into law on 21 March 1804, becoming the first great modern codification of the law. This book is a collection of essays on this notable legal achievement. Anglo-Saxon readers will find this volume especially useful, as its aim is to make the *Code* intelligible to those familiar with the common law tradition. The book covers the ideological and philosophical background of the *Code* and gives an outline of the *Code*. Among the topics discussed are codification and national unity, the *Code* and case law, techniques of interpreting the *Code*, and the *Code* in relation to contracts, the family - a section very revealing on the position of women and children in France - property, and unfair competition.

326 French administrative law and the common-law world.
Bernard Schwartz. New York: New York University Press, 1954. 367p. bibliog.

This study comparing French administrative law with English and American law should prove helpful to those wishing to grasp the fundamental principles of the French system. The administrative courts, the law courts, the public administra-

Law and Constitution

tion, review procedures, the scope of review, and the liability of the state and public officials in France are thoroughly discussed.

327 **The French Civil Code: as amended to July 1, 1976.**
Translated by John H. Crabb. South Hackensack, New Jersey: F. B. Rothman, 1977. 443p.

A book that admirably satisfies the long-felt need for a new, updated English translation of the *Code civil*.

328 **The constitutions and other select documents illustrative of the history of France, 1789-1907.**
Frank Maloy Anderson. Minneapolis, Minnesota: Wilson, 1908. 2nd ed., revised and enlarged. 693p. bibliog.
Reprinted, New York: Russell & Russell, 1967.

A collection of English translations of French laws, decrees, declarations, diplomatic papers, proclamations, addresses, treaties, and other documents of importance in French history. The first document is the 'Decree creating the National Assembly, June 17, 1789'; the last items are several 1905-07 'Documents upon the separation of church and state'. A short paragraph by the editor precedes each selection, giving the facts and context within which it was issued. The constitutions of France from 1791 to 1875 are included. Students of French history, politics, or government will find this an extremely useful book.

329 **The constitution of the Fifth Republic.**
Translated by Peter Campbell, Brian Chapman. Oxford, England: Blackwell, 1959. 61p.

'Provides a translation of the constitution of the Fifth Republic, notes comparing the final version with the government's original draft and the proposals of the Consultative Constitutional Committee, and an account of the systems for electing senators and deputies.'.

330 **The French constitution of 1958: I. The final text and its prospects.**
Stanley Hoffmann. *American Political Science Review*, vol. 43, pt. 2 (June 1959), p. 332-57.

Analyses the provisions of the constitution of the Fifth Republic 'in order to show the ways in which the drafters of the text have tried to reach their double objective: to create effective government authority in France and to establish between France and her former colonies in Africa a system of new, postcolonial relations'.

331 **The French constitution of 1958: II. The initial draft and its origins.**
Nicholas Wahl. *American Political Science Review*, vol. 43, pt. 2 (June 1959), p. 358-82.

Complements Hoffmann's article (previous item) by discussing the preparation of the government's draft of the constitution. The article is based upon information obtained from interviews with Michel Debré and his party of experts, who prepared the draft version, and from an examination of a series of working drafts.

Economics

332 **French economic growth.**
Jean-Jacques Carre, P. Dubois, E. Malinvaud, translated from the French by John P. Hatfield. Stanford, California: Stanford University Press, 1975. 581p. bibliog. (Studies in Economic Growth in Industrialized Countries).

This book covering the growth of the French economy from 1896 to 1969 is divided neatly into two sections. The first is concerned with the physical sources of economic growth - production, human resources, labour productivity, investment, growth of capital, industrial structures, total productivity, and technological progress. The second examines the causes of economic growth - demand, investment and savings, finance, economic stability, foreign trade and productivity, competition and the price system, and planning and economic information.

333 **An economic history of modern France.**
François Caron. New York: Columbia University Press, 1979. 360p.

A history of the past 160 years of capitalism as it functions in France, where the distinguishing mark of the system is the government's willingness to intervene in the economy in the name of the general welfare. The author is professor of contemporary economic history at the Sorbonne; readers will find his analysis of the revitalized French economy of the 1960s of particular interest.

334 **The social economy of France.**
Peter Coffey. New York: St. Martin's Press; London: Macmillan, 1973. 133p. bibliog.

An excellent summary of the socio-economic problems that France faced after the events of May-June 1968. As Coffey comments in his preface, 'the current attention to social policy [in France] is worthy of our interest both by the sheer novelty of some of the measures used and by the order of priorities which France has chosen'. Besides his analysis of social problems and the measures taken to solve them, Coffey describes social and economic organizations and groups in France, gives an account of the management of the French national economy, and draws qualitative and quantitative conclusions about the French standard of living.

Economics

335 **French economy and the state.**
Warren C. Baum. Princeton, New Jersey: Princeton University Press, 1958. 391p. bibliog. (Rand Corporation Research Study).

A book with a deservedly high reputation, this is the best study of the French economy from 1945 to 1957. Its focus on the government's efforts to intervene in and control the economy during this period makes the book profitable reading for political scientists as well as economists. After an excellent overview of the postwar situation, the author examines the roles that the state assumed: public financier, entrepreneur, owner of public property, and regulator of business and agriculture. Baum has succeeded in simplifying theoretical economic problems in his work, making it one of the few treatises that can be wholeheartedly recommended to the noneconomist.

336 **The growth of European mixed economies, 1945-1970: a concise study of the economic evolution of six countries.**
Sima Lieberman. Cambridge, Massachusetts: Schenkman, 1977. 347p. bibliog. (Halsted Press Book).

France was, of course, a key country in the economic recovery of Europe after the Second World War; the author devotes a sizeable proportion of his revisionist economic history to an analysis of French economic evolution. His first chapter covers France from 1945 to 1955, discussing the Monnet Plan, 1947-52, the Hirsch Plan, 1951-57, problems of trade unions, politics, and inflation, and causes of economic growth. A later chapter takes up the post-1955 French economy with an analysis of the economic changes of the De Gaulle-Pompidou era.

337 **Economic planning in France.**
John Hackett, Anne-Marie Hackett. London: Allen & Unwin; Cambridge, Massachusetts: Harvard University Press, 1963. 418p. maps. bibliog.

The authors wrote this book in 1963, after the French had completed nearly two decades of planning, from the First Plan of 1947-52 to the inception of the Fourth Plan in 1962. Written especially for an Anglo-Saxon readership, it remains a basic source for information on planning in France, systematically covering all aspects of the subject.

338 **Economic planning: the French experience.**
Pierre Bauchet, translated from the French by Daphne Woodward. New York: Praeger, 1964. 299p.

A book that covers the same time period as the Hacketts' (previous item), but from the perspective of a French economist who has been involved in the process that he describes. The author presents the motives, aims, and difficulties involved in drafting and implementing the plan. He details the mechanism of planning, and relates the planning process to government and to industrial groups.

Economics

339 **Modern capitalist planning: the French model.**
Stephen S. Cohen. Berkeley, California: University of California Press; London: Weidenfeld & Nicolson, 1969. 334p. bibliog.

After the Second World War, France adopted a 'mixed economy', commencing her First Plan in 1947. In this recent publication, the author studies the plan in the framework of modern capitalism, tracing its social and historical evolution and examining its role in the political economy. He does not hesitate to generalize from his facts: his conclusion is that adoption of the plan concept is leading France towards corporatism.

340 **Internal migration and regional economic growth: a case study of France.**
A. Fielding. *Urban Studies*, vol. 3, pt. 3 (Nov. 1966), p. 200-14.

A study of the mobility of the population in France: 'Attention is concentrated in this paper on the influence of regional economic growth in determining the character and direction of internal migration flows'.

341 **Economic surveys: France.**
Paris: Organization for Economic Co-operation and Development, 1953-, irregular.

A detailed survey of the market economy of France, this publication is a major source for statistics and analysis concerning demand, production, wages and prices, conditions in the money and capital markets, and developments in the balance of payments. Since France is a member of the OECD, the state of the French economy in relation to the world receives coverage in the OECD's specialized periodicals that provide comparative economic data: *OECD Economic Outlook* (1967-, semi-annual); *Main Economic Indicators* (monthly); and *Statistics of Foreign Trade, Series A* (1974-, monthly) and *Series B* (1974-, quarterly).

342 **French mercantilist doctrines before Colbert.**
C. W. Cole. New York: Columbia University Press, 1931. 243p. bibliog. Reprinted, New York: Octagon, 1969.

The first volume of the author's standard work on the mercantilist period of France's economic history; it was followed by *Colbert and a century of French mercantilism* (New York, 1939) and *French mercantilism, 1683-1700* (New York, 1943. Reprinted, New York: Octagon, 1965).

343 **International economy and monetary movements in France, 1493-1725.**
Frank C. Spooner. Cambridge, Massachusetts: Harvard University Press, 1972. 354p. bibliog. (Harvard Economic Studies, 138).

A recent, thoroughgoing study of early French monetary policy and international trade movements. A highly technical presentation that will probably be of interest to the specialist or economic historian.

Economics

344 France: a history of national economics, 1789-1939.
S. B. Clough. New York: Scribner's, 1939. 498p. bibliog.
Reprinted, New York: Octagon Books, 1964.

In this often-cited work, the author discusses the 'national [economic] problems of France in their historical setting', tracing them from the 1789 revolutionary reforms to the 1930s. The book is both an analysis and a history of French economic development within this period.

345 Economic growth in France and Britain, 1851-1950.
Charles P. Kindleberger. Cambridge, Massachusetts: Harvard University Press, 1964. 378p. bibliog.

A synthesis and a critique, by a very well known scholar, of the models that have been developed in order to explain the course of economic growth in France and Britain during the hundred years stretching from the Second Empire into the Fourth Republic. Placing the emphasis on France, the author examines resources, capital, population, social determinants, entrepreneurship, technology, industrial scale, business competition, government intervention, agricultural transformation, urbanization, and foreign trade in order to isolate the significant factors that would explain the economic positions of the two countries.

346 Essays in French economic history.
Edited by Rondo Cameron, with the assistance of F. F. Mendels, J. P. Ward. Homewood, Illinois: R. D. Irwin, 1970. 423p. bibliog.

Economic history is currently one of the most active intellectual disciplines in France: this collection of essays by French economic historians will be welcomed by Anglo-Saxon readers seeking an orientation to the field. The editor has arranged the book as a guide for students: after an introductory survey tracing the development of economic historiography in France, the essays are presented chronologically, with each section - ancient to 20th century - having its own introduction. The appendix 'Orientation to research' lists and discusses materials available both in France and in the United States for those who wish to pursue work in the subject.

347 Inflation and unemployment in France: a quantitative analysis.
Jan Marczewski, translated from the French by Marian Reeds. New York: Praeger, 1978. 200p. (Praeger Special Studies).

The author states that 'inflation is the most important general and economic problem in France today'. And, although many studies have been devoted to inflation, Marczewski, an economics professor at the Sorbonne, believes there remains a gap in the literature that his book can fill: a need for 'research which approaches the phenomenon of inflation from the standpoint of the broadest possible set of economic relationships that might concern it directly or indirectly in time and space'. Data and conclusions are presented in a technical fashion, making this a book for the specialist.

Economics

348 **The Common Market and how it works.**
Anthony J. C. Kerr. Oxford, England; New York: Pergamon Press, 1977. 210p. bibliog.

Since France is first in size and politically the most important member of the European Economic Community, the student of contemporary France will wish to understand something of the aims, policies, and structure of this complex organization. This book is a good introduction to the EEC, providing historical background and basic details for its member states, outlining the Community's major institutions, its decision-making processes and its policies, and giving an account of its position in relation to industry and technology, developing countries, financial affairs, credits and investments, internal trade, education, and science.

Finance and Banking

349 **The European money puzzle.**
Peter Readman, with Jonathan Davies, Michael H. D. Pode. London: Michael Joseph, 1973. 164p.
A book about continental finance directed specifically at the British reader. The twenty-page chapter on the French financial system is a nontechnical summary of the situation in France, where the government exerts a high degree of control on the money market. Savings and credit institutions, life insurance companies, and the bond and equity markets are described. A helpful diagram of the financial institutional structure is included.

350 **Competition and controls in banking: a study of the regulation of bank competition in Italy, France, and England.**
David Alhadeff. Berkeley, California: University of California Press, 1968. 384p. bibliog. (Institute of Business and Economic Research and Institute of Industrial Relations, University of California, Berkeley).
The author states in his preface that he hopes to fill a gap in the literature of European banking by focusing on the regulatory frameworks within which European banks operate. The part of the book devoted to France includes an overview of the French banking structure, details on government regulations and monetary controls, and an analysis of the effects of such controls on the banking market.

351 **French banking structure and credit policy.**
J. S. G. Wilson. London: Bell, for the London School of Economics; Cambridge, Massachusetts: Harvard University Press, 1957. 453p. bibliog.
A standard work on French finance and banking. Covers the country's financial institutions, deposit and investment banking, and private banks. The entire second half of the book is devoted to the Banque de France.

Business and Industry

352 **Organized business in France.**
Henry W. Ehrmann. Princeton, New Jersey: Princeton University Press, 1957. 514p. bibliog.

A study of the activities of the French employers' association - the Conseil National de Patronat and its predecessor the Confédération Générale de la Production Française - as an organized lobby and pressure group seeking to obtain and wield political power. The relations of this group with the government, with industrial trade unions, and with other interprofessional groups are scrutinized, and its attitudes and policies on economic and social issues defined. An interesting chapter covers organized business under the Vichy régime.

353 **Promotion and control of industry in postwar France.**
John Sheahan. Cambridge, Massachusetts: Harvard University Press, 1963. 301p. bibliog.

'This present study aims at an exploration in detail of choices in the area of governmental and private control of industry. It emphasizes contrasts between the organization of particular industries in France and the United States and attempts to trace out some of their major consequences for performance. It is focused on the manufacturing sector and on the decade from 1950 to 1960'. The industries discussed are the aluminium, steel, industrial equipment, automobile, and cotton textile industries.

354 **Managerial comparisons of four developed countries: France, Britain, United States, Russia.**
David Granick. Cambridge, Massachusetts: MIT Press, 1972. 394p. bibliog.

Discusses styles of management in large-scale nongovernmental manufacturing firms, focusing on how value systems and incentive schemes influence managerial behaviour. The emphasis is on Britain and France, comparing them to each other and to the USA and the USSR. The interviews on which the book is based were conducted from 1963 to 1968.

Business and Industry

355 **Political strategies for industrial order: state, market, and industry in France.**
John Zysman. Berkeley, California: University of California Press, 1977. 230p.

Although this book focuses on the electronics industry, the author's purpose is to analyse government-industrial relations in France in a broad context. The preface states that three themes are developed: 'The links between technological change and social development; the relations between political and economic activity, specifically the organizational and economic consequences of particular relations between business and the state; and the role of the nation-state in mediating the priorities of the national economy in a global economic order'.

356 **French economy has a chill.**
Andrew Lloyd. *Electronics*, vol. 51, pt. 1 (5 Jan. 1978), p. 108-9.

A brief report on the French electronics industry that predicts slowed-down growth, more inflation, and more unemployment for 1978. A chart sums up production for 1976 and 1977 and projects 1978 figures for the industry.

357 **Industrial policies in Western Europe.**
Edited by Steven J. Warnecke, Ezra N. Suleiman. New York: Praeger, 1975. 249p. bibliog. (Praeger Special Studies in International Politics and Government).

This volume of essays on national and private industrial policies in the countries of the European Economic Community provides much factual information on policies followed in France's petroleum, textile, and electronics industries.

358 **Enterprise and entrepreneurs in nineteenth- and twentieth-century France.**
Edward C. Carter, II, Robert Forster, Joseph Moody. Baltimore, Maryland: Johns Hopkins Press, 1976. 207p.

A collection of four essays, originally given as lectures, on various aspects of modern business history in France. The essays and their authors are: 'Technical education and the French entrepreneur' (C. P. Kindleberger); 'Religion and enterprise' (D. Landes); 'Innovation and business strategies in nineteenth- and twentieth-century France' (M. Levy-Leboyer); and 'Entrepreneurial patronage in nineteenth-century France' (A. Boime).

359 **In first gear: the French automobile industry to 1914.**
James M. Laux. Montreal, Canada: McGill-Queen's University Press, 1976. 256p.

A fascinating survey of the beginnings of this important French industry, by a historian.

Fashion

360 **Couture: an illustrated history of the great Paris designers and their creations.**
Edited by Ruth Lynam. Garden City, New York: Doubleday, 1972. 256p.
The history of the world of Parisian *haute couture* from its mid-19th century beginnings with Englishman Charles Frederick Worth to the 1970s. Separate chapters are devoted to the top designers: Chanel, Dior, Fath, Courrèges and Ungaro, Cardin, and Saint-Laurent. The reader is given an inside look at the trade, including a description of the fashion organization, the Chambre Syndicale de la Couture Parisienne. An essay by model Penelope Portrait depicts the world of the high-fashion mannequin of the 1950s. The book is well illustrated with photographs of the designers and their creations.

361 **World of fashion: people, places, resources.**
Eleanor Lambert. New York: Bowker, 1976. 361p. bibliog.
A new and useful reference source that gathers together the facts on fashion in each country of the world. The pages devoted to France contain a brief summary of 'its current contribution to modern dress', followed by directory listings of fashion designers and firms, fashion arbiters, trade associations, educational institutions, and costume and fashion archives.

Trade Unions and Labour Movements

362 **The French labor movement.**
Val Lorwin. Cambridge, Massachusetts: Harvard University Press, 1954. 346p. bibliog. (Wertheim Publications in Industrial Relations).

This book, although written in 1954, retains first place among histories of the French labour movement. Arranged in three parts, the first two sections continue to be the best studies of the development of the unions from 1789 to 1953. (The third section, analysing union structure and politics as of 1953 is, of course, out of date). The book includes an appendix that gives a chronology of labour developments with parallel political events, 1789-1953, and a selection of important labour documents.

363 **French labor from Popular Front to Liberation.**
Henry W. Ehrmann. New York: Oxford University Press, 1947. 329p. bibliog. Reprinted, New York: Russell, 1971.

This well-written history of French labour, 1934-44, continues to be valuable, and librarians will be pleased to see it reprinted. The work is based on primary sources and is in some respects a sequel to *The labor movement in post-war France*, by David Saposs (New York: Columbia University Press, 1931. Reprinted, New York: Russell, 1972).

364 **A bibliography of French labor, with a selection of documents on the French labor movement.**
Leon A. Dale. New York: Kelley, 1969. 317p. (Reprints of Economic Classics).

Despite the series in which it is included, this is not a reprint, but a work first published in 1969. It is an unannotated list of books about French labour from 1600 to 1969, and of significant newspaper and magazine articles on the subject appearing during the same period. It also includes a list of the most important newspapers and magazines concerned with the labour movement. The majority of

Trade Unions and Labour Movements

the works are in French or English. Ten documents, chosen as being representative of the French labour movement's history, are reprinted in the book.

365 The origins of the French labor movement: the socialism of skilled workers, 1830-1906.
Bernard H. Moss. Berkeley, California: University of California Press, 1976. 217p. bibliog.

A study of socialist ideology and its relationship to the working class, by an author who sets as his aim the rehabilitation of ideology 'both as a vital force in history and as a serious subject for historical inquiry'. The bibliographical essay appended to the main text is an excellent summary and evaluation of scholarly work on the French labour movement.

366 Revolutionary syndicalism in France: the direct action of its time.
F. F. Ridley. London: Cambridge University Press, 1970. 279p. bibliog.

Revolutionary syndicalism in France was a movement that set itself against the liberal-bourgeois state and its law. It was a movement that combined many diverse elements - unionism, anarchism, and revolutionary aspirations. It was antiparliamentarian, antidemocratic, antirational, and antibourgeois, and made a cult of 'direct action' and the general strike. This book is a sympathetic account of the movement that discusses both its history and its political theory.

367 Revolutionary syndicalism and French labor: a cause without rebels.
Peter N. Stearns. New Brunswick, New Jersey: Rutgers University Press, 1971. 175p.

Another recent study of French syndicalism, written to question the ordinary worker's acceptance of the ideology of syndicalist leaders in the 1890-1914 period. The author approaches syndicalism from historical, psychological, and sociological perspectives and analyses its failure. He concludes that syndicalism was a good protest doctrine, but fated to be sterile outside the realm of theory.

368 Strikes in France, 1830-1968.
Edward Shorter, Charles Tilly. London, New York: Cambridge University Press, 1974. 428p. bibliog.

A comprehensive study of 140 years of strikes in France, during which time labour actions have altered the basic objectives for which they are undertaken. Readers may find this book somewhat daunting in its statistical approach, but librarians will certainly wish to include it in library collections.

369 Reform of the enterprise in France.
Y. Delamotte. *Annals of the American Academy of Political and Social Science*, vol. 431 (May 1977), p. 54-62.

'Reform of the enterprise' is the French phrase for 'industrial democracy'. This article, included in a volume of the *Annals of the American Academy of Political and Social Science* entitled 'Industrial democracy in international perspective', deals with recent attempts by the French to institute reforms in industry, and is

Trade Unions and Labour Movements

in large part a consideration of the 1975 Sudreau Report, an examination of the French situation undertaken at the request of the French government. The chief proposals of the report are given and the possibility of their implementation by French industry discussed.

Agriculture

370 **French rural history: an essay on its basic characteristics.**
Marc Bloch, translated from the French by Janet Sondheimer. Berkeley, California: University of California Press, 1966. 258p. bibliog.

Bloch's classic study of agrarian history, published in 1931, has been called 'a masterpiece of historical detection', and 'a model of imaginative reconstruction'. Data and conclusions in this area of French history have, of course, been revised since Bloch's work appeared, but much of the book is still pertinent. This competently translated edition has a helpful preface by Bloch's colleague and cofounder of the *Annales* School, Lucien Febvre.

371 **The winegrowers of France and the government since 1875.**
Charles K. Warner. New York: Columbia University Press, 1960. 303p. maps. bibliog.

'After 1875, when the destructive phylloxera epidemic first hit the French vineyards in force, the relative value of wine to the economy began to decline. The succeeding crises that accompanied this decline and the role that the government played in trying to check them form the subject of this study'.

372 **Agricultural productivity and economic development in France, 1852-1950, with the revised French version.**
Louis M. Goreux. New York: Arno Press, 1977. 376p. bibliog. (Dissertations in European Economic History).

A detailed study originally written as the author's thesis at the University of Chicago in 1955.

Agriculture

373 **Rural revolution in France: the peasantry in the twentieth century.**
Gordon Wright. Stanford, California: Stanford University Press, 1964. 271p. maps.

A highly regarded basic source on the transformation of rural conditions in France since the Third Republic.

Transport

374 **Road of the toll.**
J. N. Tuppen. *Geographical Magazine* (London), vol. 49 (May 1977), p. 483-6.

A short article written on the occasion of the completion of the *Autoroute de l'Est* between Paris and West Germany. The author discusses both the national and international significance of this event, noting that the establishment of a direct link between French and West German highway systems is an important milestone in the integration of the trade and communications of EEC countries.

375 **The Concorde conspiracy: the international race for the SST.**
John Costello, Terry Hughes. New York: Scribner's, 1976. 302p.

This popular account of the development and marketing of the supersonic transport aircraft, the Anglo-French Concorde 002, gives the reader a close look at ties between industry, politics, and economics.

376 **French railroads and the state.**
Kimon A. Doukas. New York: Columbia University Press, 1945. 287p. bibliog. (Studies in History, Economics and Public Law, no. 517). Reprinted, New York: Octagon Books, 1972.

It is gratifying to see reprinted this thorough study of the relationship of the French railroads to the state during the century 1823-1937. The relation of the railroad industry to national defence and to the national economy are only two of the topics covered in this volume, originally presented as the author's thesis at Columbia University.

Environment

377 **Greener than thou.**
Economist (London), no. 6967, vol. 262 (12 March 1977), p. 58.
A brief discussion of environmentalism in France in the context of the 1977 Paris Mayoral election and a possible 'ecology vote'. Written by the magazine's Paris correspondent, the article comments that the new movement 'mixes Douanier Rousseau pastoral ideals with Ralph Nader aggression', and that 'consumer awareness has come later to France than to any other industrial nation'.

378 **Energy and the European communities.**
Nigel J. D. Lucas. London: Europa Publishers, 1977. 175p.
France is included among the countries dealt with in this detailed appraisal of European Economic Community energy policy. The history of Community energy policy is covered, present policies evaluated, and suggestions for future policy made.

379 **French energy plan for 1985.**
Thomas C. Ponder. *Hydrocarbon Processing*, vol. 56, pt. 5 (May 1977), p. 56.
This article is based on 'Guide lines for French energy policy until 1985', a paper by R. M. Doumec originally presented at Valley Forge, Pennsylvania, October 1976. It gives a concise overview and a nontechnical discussion of the current French energy situation, projects future needs, and considers the possibilities for satisfying such needs. 'With increasing emphasis on nuclear [energy], a definite conservation program, and a planned growth of 5 per cent, France must import 60 per cent of her energy needs through 1985'.

380 **Coping with the oil crisis: French and German experiences.**
Horst Mendershausen. Baltimore, Maryland: Johns Hopkins University Press, 1976. 110p.
Mendershausen combines economic and political analysis in this case study of the responses of France and the Federal Republic of Germany to the oil crisis that followed the Middle East War of October 1973. He describes, compares, and

Environment

contrasts the origins and evolution of the policies that these governments developed in reaction to the breakdown of the international order in oil, and places them in the context of the global situation.

381 **Recherche sur la pollution atmosphérique: 1972-1975.** (Air pollution research: 1972-75.)
Edited by Paul Chovin, Jean-Claude Oppeneau. Neuilly, France: Service des Affaires Scientifiques, 1977. 165p. (Recherche Environnement, 4).

A report on programmes dealing with France's air pollution problems. The main text is in French, with summaries in English.

Food and Drink

382 The food of France.
Waverley Root.   New York: Knopf, 1958. 486p.

A book that whets the appetite for France as well as for French cooking. Not a book of recipes but a 'gastronomic exploration of France' - besides accounts of food, the reader will find much entertaining, factual information on French geography and history. The author is an acute observer and knows France thoroughly: his book has won the right to be called the 'definitive treatise' on French food.

383 The New Larousse gastronomique.
Edited by Janet Dunbar, translated from the French by Marion Hunter, American edition edited by Charlotte Turgeon,   New York: Crown, 1977. 1104p.

A revised edition of the famous cookery book, of interest not only for its 8,500 international recipes but also as a source of information on French cuisine and culinary terms.

384 The Escoffier cook book: a guide to the fine art of cookery.
Auguste Escoffier.   New York: Crown, 1969. Reprinted, 1977. 923p.

The American edition of the French master chef's *Guide culinaire*; recipes are translated into American terms and usage. The first part of the book discusses the fundamental elements of cooking; the second part, the bulk of the book, contains the recipes. The volume includes a glossary of French cooking terms.

385 The wines and vineyards of France.
Louis Jacquelin, Rene Poulain, translated from the French by T. A. Layton.   New York: Putnam's, 1960. 416p. maps.

An authoritative reference volume by two distinguished French oenologists. The vineyards and the wines of France are described in detail. The introduction includes a knowledgeable discussion by the translator of the literature on wine in English and French.

Food and Drink

386 **Wines of France.**
Alexis Lichine. New York: Knopf, 1969. 5th rev. ed. 337p. maps.

A comprehensive, periodically revised compendium on French wines that includes a chapter on the brandies, cognac and armagnac. The appendix gives information on buying, storing, serving, and drinking wine.

387 **Champagne: with appendices on corks, methods of keeping and serving champagne, vintages, brands, shippers.**
André L. Simon. London: Constable, 1934. 140p.
(Constable's Wine Library).

A practical handbook by an acknowledged expert. The author traces the history of France's most distinctive wine from the 17th century to the 20th. The appendix gives the rules for keeping, drinking, and serving champagne: 'Champagne *must* be kept in a flat or horizontal position *always*'.

388 **A history of champagne: with notes on the other sparkling wines.**
Henry Vizetelly. London: Vizetelly & Co., 1882. 263p.

A vintage history of the wine of Champagne, illustrated with 350 engravings. The author recounts facts and legends, beginning with 'the vine in Gaul', and ending with the Victorian dinner party.

389 **The breads of France.**
Bernard Clayton, Jr. New York: Bobbs-Merrill, 1979. 284p.

A recipe book that can also serve as a reference source for information on one of the delights of French cuisine. Includes recipes for regional specialities, as well as for the classic baguettes and croissants.

Science and Technology

390 **French science and its principal discoveries since the seventeenth century.**
Maurice Caullery. New York: [French Institute], 1934. 229p. Reprinted, New York: Arno Press, 1975.

Despite the considerable role that France played in the creation of modern science, this short account remains the only general history of French science from the 1600s to the 1920s available in English. Chapters outline the discoveries and advances of French science and technology during this period, including the work of inventors as well as that of creators.

391 **The Society of Arcueil: a view of French science at the time of Napoleon.**
Maurice Crosland. London: Heinemann, 1967. 514p. bibliog. (Heinemann Books on the History of Science).

A well-documented history and appraisal of the scientific activities of the Society of Arcueil during its heyday under Napoleon Bonaparte, written with the aim of drawing some conclusions as to the state of French science during the early 19th century. As the author states in his preface, for the historian of science, 'the period of Napoleon Bonaparte's rise to power is one of exceptional interest, and although the familiar political and military history must be put to one side, the effect of the political scene on the men of science, and their contribution to the national economy of France, may not be the least interesting aspect to emerge [from this study]'.

392 **The emergence of science in Western Europe.**
Edited by Maurice Crosland. New York: Science History Publications, 1976. 201p.

A book that contains two informative chapters on early French science by distinguished historians of science. R. Hahn writes about 'Scientific careers in eigh-

Science and Technology

teenth-century France', and M. Crosland discusses early 19th-century France in 'The development of a professional career in science in France'.

393 **France in the age of the scientific state.**
R. Gilpin. Princeton, New Jersey: Princeton University Press, 1968. 474p. map. bibliog.

According to the author, the new role of science and technology in human affairs has had far-reaching consequences for the European nation-state. His book centres on France's problems as she seeks to 'transform herself into a scientific nation-state on the models of the United States and the Union of Soviet Socialist Republics, without ceasing to be herself'.

394 **European advanced technology: a programme for integration.**
Christopher Layton. London: Allen & Unwin, 1969. 293p. bibliog.

This book, directed towards a British audience, focuses on European efforts to integrate scientific and technological activities and programmes. The volume is both interesting and informative on France's aerospace, aviation, communications, and defence industries, on her nuclear programme, and on the English Channel Tunnel project.

395 **French inventions of the eighteenth-century.**
Shelby T. McCloy. Lexington, Kentucky: University of Kentucky Press, 1952. 212p. bibliog.

The first book in English to cover the rich inventive activity that took place in 18th century France. A well-researched piece of work, based on both primary and secondary sources, it surveys the whole field: the balloon, steam transportation, telegraphy, lighting, papermaking, chemical inventions, textiles, automata, military inventions, and medical and surgical innovations. The last two chapters discuss the relationship between the inventor and Enlightenment society.

396 **The scientist's role in society: a comparative study.**
Joseph Ben-David. Englewood Cliffs, New Jersey: Prentice-Hall, 1971. 207p. (Foundations of Modern Sociology series).

A book that focuses on the emergence and development of the social role of the scientist from a comparative and historical perspective. In a chapter entitled 'The rise and decline of the French scientific center in a regime of centralized liberalism', Ben-David discusses the reasons for the French leadership of world science during the first three decades of the 19th century, and seeks an explanation for France's subsequent loss of this role. An appendix gives tables of figures comparing scientific productivity in France, Germany, Great Britain, and the United States.

397 **Guide to the industrial archaeology of Europe.**
Kenneth Hudson. Madison, New Jersey: Fairleigh Dickinson University Press, 1971. 186p.

This guidebook to technological and industrial monuments locates 'material relating to yesterday's manufacturing and transport which has survived, more or less intact, on its original site'. The section devoted to France lists and locates

Science and Technology

museums of industrial and technical history, saltworks, windmills, bridges, aqueducts, canals, railways, docks, factories, collieries, and foundries.

398 **French medicine.**
M. Laignel-Lavastine, Raymond Molinery, translated from the French by E. B. Krumbhaar. New York: Hoeber, 1934. 187p. (Clio Medica, 15). Reprinted, New York: AMS Press, 1978.

A brief volume that traces the history of medicine in France from the days of the Gauls' medical magicians to the first decades of the 20th century. The latter part of the book deals with modern medicine and focuses on the contributions of the great names in French medicine and biological research: Bichat, Claude Bernard, Laennec, and Pasteur.

399 **The medicine show: patients, physicians and the perplexities of the health revolution in modern society.**
Edited by Patricia Branca. New York: Science History Publications/U.S.A., 1977. 280p. bibliog.

The four essays on the social history of medicine in France that are collected in this volume focus on the doctor as an agent of social change and on the professionalization of the medical profession. The essays and their authors are: 'Medical power and popular medicine: illegal healers in nineteenth-century France' (Matthew Ramsey); 'The extent of medical practice in France around 1780' (Jean-Pierre Goubert); 'Thomas Herier, a country surgeon outside Angoulême at the end of the XVIIIth century' (Edna Hindle Lemay); and 'Physicians in Lyon during the nineteenth century' (Olivier Faure).

Language

General

400 A history of the French language.
Peter Rickard. London: Hutchinson, 1974. 174p. bibliog.
A succinct presentation of the evolution of the French language from Vulgar Latin to its present form. The author outlines the dominant trends and the significant developments in the language without going into too much detail. The book also contains a list of the countries where French is either the official language, one of the official languages, or widely spoken.

401 A glossary of French literary expression.
James Redfern. New York: Harcourt, Brace & World, 1970. unpaginated. bibliog.
A volume that should prove useful for students of French literature engaged in writing criticism. Presupposing a college-level achievement in French, the author states that his aim is 'to present the elements of a basic critical vocabulary in contexts which can serve as models of expression for the students' own ideas'. A word is listed, then used in a sentence. At the end of the volume is a list of adjectives derived from proper names.

402 French reference grammar for schools and colleges.
J. E. Mansion. London, New York: D. C. Heath, 1928. 2nd ed. maps. 247p. Reprinted, Westport, Connecticut: Greenwood Press, 1971.
A handy, well-known reference grammar that presents the rules of French syntax clearly and comprehensively.

Language. Dictionaries

403 **Your guide to French pronunciation.**
Monique Bras. Paris: Larousse, 1975. 231p.
This is a step-by-step workbook written by a teacher with many years experience in teaching French to English-speakers. It is designed particularly for those speaking American English.

Dictionaries

404 **Larousse modern French-English, English-French dictionary.**
Edited by M. M. Dubois. Paris: Larousse; New York: McGraw-Hill, 1960. 768, 751p.
One of the most widely used one-volume bilingual dictionaries. Contains illustrations, vocabulary charts, and a summary of French grammar.

405 **Harrap's shorter French and English dictionary.**
J. E. Mansion, revised by M. Ferlin, P. Forbes, edited by D. M. Ledesert, R. P. Ledesert. London, Toronto: Harrap, 1967. Completely revised and enlarged ed. 1489p.
Another excellent single-volume bilingual dictionary, whose 97,000 entries are selected from the reliable *Harrap's standard.*

406 **Le gimmick: français parlé.** (The gimmick: spoken French.)
Adrienne. New York: Norton, 1977. 2nd rev. ed. 185p.
A necessity for those who wish to express themselves colloquially in French: provides the French equivalents for American and English everyday expressions - including taboo words.

407 **French-English science and technology dictionary.**
Louis De Vries, revised and enlarged by Stanley Hochman. New York: McGraw-Hill, 1976. 4th ed. 683p.
A dictionary of the terms used in agricultural, biological and physical sciences. De Vries's dictionary has been published since 1940 and is consistently updated; the 4th edition has a supplement of 4,500 new terms in aeronautics, astronautics, atomic energy, automobile technology, electronic data processing, electronics, nuclear science and technology, radar, radio, and television. For each French word, the English equivalent is given. Abbreviations appear in a separate section at the back of the volume.

Literature

General

408 **Concise bibliography of French literature.**
Denis Mahaffey. New York: Bowker, 1975. 286p.
An up-to-date bibliographical guide to French literature, from the 842 *Serments de Strasbourg* to 1960. The author arranges his material first into six period divisions, then alphabetically by author. For each writer, the reader will find listed editions, standard translations, and major bibliographical, biographical, and critical works. Entries give bibliographical details only - no annotations.

409 **A book of French quotations with English translations.**
Norbert Guterman. Garden City, New York: Doubleday, 1963. 442p.
The quotations included in this book cover the whole range of French literature from the 11th century *Vie de Saint Alexis* to the writings of Albert Camus. The entries are arranged so that the French selection on the left-hand page faces its English translation on the right. Short notes preceding each translation give biographical or historical information explaining the context within which the selection was written. The volume is indexed by authors and by first lines in both languages.

410 **A short history of French literature.**
Geoffrey Brereton. Harmondsworth, England; Baltimore, Maryland: Penguin Books, 1976. 2nd ed. 368p. bibliog.
Those desiring an introduction to French literature could not do better than to obtain this handy paperback volume. The whole spectrum of French literature is covered, from the *chansons de geste* to the 20th century theatre, with literary developments illuminatingly related to social events.

Literature. History and criticism

411 **French literature: its history and meaning.**
Wallace Fowlie. Englewood Cliffs, New Jersey: Prentice-Hall, 1973. 341p. bibliog.

A distinguished scholar-critic interprets the history of French literature from the Middle Ages to 1970.

412 **Women writers in France: variations on a theme.**
Germaine Bree. New Brunswick, New Jersey: Rutgers University Press, 1973. 90p. bibliog. (Brown and Haley Lectures, 1973).

When this book was reviewed in *Choice* in 1974, the reviewer commented: 'Brief as it is, [this book] is the only survey of the fortunes and accomplishments of a long tradition of successful and skillful woman writers in France from the medieval period to the "uncertain present"'.

History and criticism

413 **Medieval French literature.**
Jessie Crosland. New York: Macmillan, 1956. 266p. bibliog.

A work that concentrates on the literature of the 12th and 13th centuries, covering didactic literature, lyric poetry, the romantic epic, the *chanson de geste*, chronicles and history, the drama, and animal literature. Representative works are accorded detailed treatment. Unfortunately, selections are not translated, lessening the usefulness of this book for the non-French reader.

414 **The medieval imagination.**
Douglas Kelly. Madison, Wisconsin: University of Wisconsin Press, 1978. 416p.

A recent examination and survey of Middle French courtly literature, a segment of French literature that has been largely neglected by scholars. The author elucidates particular works and provides fresh insights into the art of the period. Although the book is written for the student of mediaeval literature, selections have been translated into English, and the informed general reader will also enjoy this book.

415 **Classical voices: studies of Corneille, Racine, Molière, Mme. de Lafayette.**
Peter H. Nurse. London: Harrap, 1971. 230p. bibliog.

Although this is a study of the four great classic French writers, the author's perspective is broad enough to include 'conventions, influences, and the sociopolitical environment' within which they wrote. The works around which the book centres are Corneille's *Horace*; Racine's *Andromaque, Britannicus*, and *Phèdre*; Molière's *Tartuffe, L'École des Femmes*, and *Don Juan*; and Madame de Lafayette's *La Princesse de Clèves*.

Literature. History and criticism

416 **Counterparts: the dynamics of Franco-German literary relationships, 1770-1895.**
Lilian R. Furst. Detroit, Michigan: Wayne State University Press, 1977. 201p. bibliog.

The author examines Romanticism as it evolved in 19th century France and Germany, and draws some interesting conclusions about the relationships between the forms that the movement took in the two nations. In her opinion, the German counterpart of French Romanticism was the Storm and Stress movement, while the French counterpart of German Romanticism was Symbolism. Her skill in explaining the dynamics of these related movements makes this book a thought-provoking work.

417 **The French novel: from Eighteen Hundred to the present.**
Winifried Engler, translated from the German by Alexander Gode. New York: Ungar, 1969. Revised and enlarged ed. 286p. bibliog.

A minutely categorized study of the French novel of the 19th and 20th centuries. Students will find that this book is helpful in giving them an overview of the genre.

418 **Style in the French novel.**
Stephen Ullmann. London: Cambridge University Press, 1957. 272p. bibliog.

This sharply focused analysis of the 19th and early 20th century French novel looks at literary texts from a linguistic viewpoint derived from the science of style. If this approach seems a bit daunting to the reader, let it be said that the book will repay an effort on his part: the author's method gets into the texture of the individual writer's work, and furnishes valuable insights into the novels of Stendhal, Mérimée, Hugo, the Goncourts, Flaubert, and Proust.

419 **The militant hackwriter; French popular literature 1800-1848: its influence, artistic and political.**
Lucian W. Minor. Bowling Green, Ohio: Ohio University Popular Press, 1975. 177p. bibliog.

A valuable study of the origins and growth of the popular novel and melodrama in France in the half-century preceding the Revolution of 1848. The author attaches artistic and political import to these phenomena of mass culture; not only did these subliterary genres influence more sophisticated literary presentations - notably Balzac - but they played a political role.

420 **The development of French Romanticism: the impact of the industrial revolution on literature.**
A. J. George. Syracuse, New York: Syracuse University Press, 1955. 193p. Reprinted, Westport, Connecticut: Greenwood Press, 1977.

Discusses the literary developments of the 1800-52 period, arguing that the Romanticism of the era stemmed from the realignments of society that resulted from the Industrial Revolution.

Literature. History and criticism

421 Bohemian versus bourgeois: French society and the French man of letters in the nineteenth century.
Cesar Grana. New York: Basic Books, 1964. 220p. bibliog.
A book of interest to the social historian as well as the literary, this is a sociological analysis of the literary period that corresponds roughly to the July Monarchy, during which, according to the author, 'the tradition of unresolvable tension between society and the man of letters became visibly entrenched'. The first part of the book describes French society under the bourgeois monarch; the second part concentrates on those aspects of the work of Stendhal, Flaubert, and Baudelaire which place them in the tradition of critics of the middle class. A paperback edition of this work entitled *Modernity and its discontents* is available (New York: Harper & Row, 1967).

422 The gates of horn: a study of five French realists.
Harry Levin. New York: Oxford University Press, 1963. 554p.
A superior study of five French novelists - Stendhal, Balzac, Flaubert, Zola, and Proust - who made decisive contributions to French literature in their conscious pursuit of 'reality'. The author clarifes their perspectives, pointing out what 'reality' meant to each. He describes the strategies these writers adopted in order to deflate and reexamine received opinion, and the techniques they utilized to transfer their visions to the printed page.

423 Nineteenth-century French Romantic poets.
Robert T. Denomme. Carbondale, Illinois: Southern Illinois University Press; London: Feffer & Simons, 1969. 176p. bibliog. (Crosscurrents/Modern Critiques).
An appraisal and critical survey of Romanticism in France. The author defines Romanticism in an introduction, then discusses the works of the major French Romantics: Lamartine, Vigny, Hugo, and Musset.

424 The French Parnassian poets.
Robert T. Denomme. Carbondale, Illinois: Southern Illinois University Press; London: Feffer & Simons, 1972. 150p. bibliog. (Crosscurrents/Modern Critiques).
An informative study of the 19th century poets - Gautier, de Banville, Leconte de Lisle, Heredia - who opposed Romanticism.

425 The language of French symbolism.
James Lawler. Princeton, New Jersey: Princeton University Press, 1969. 270p. bibliog.
The author draws on linguistic concepts to elucidate the poetic practices of the six men central to the 1870-1920 French Symbolist movement: Mallarmé, Verlaine, Rimbaud, Claudel, Valéry, and Apollinaire.

Literature. Contemporary

426 **The modern movement: one hundred key books from England, France, and America, 1880-1950.**
Cyril Connolly. New York: Atheneum, 1966. 148p.
French writers figure prominently in this bibliography of books that embody the modern spirit, defined by the author as 'a combination of certain intellectual qualities inherited from the Enlightenment: lucidity, irony, scepticism, intellectual curiosity, combined with the passionate intensity of the Romantics, their rebellion and sense of technical experiment, their awareness of living in a tragic age'. Each book receives an informative paragraph, describing the work and situating it in the modern movement.

427 **An anthology of modern French poetry (1850-1950).**
Edited by Peter Broome, Graham Chesters. London, New York: Cambridge University Press, 1976. 208p.
Poems by Hugo, Nerval, Baudelaire, Mallarmé, Cros, Verlaine, Rimbaud, Laforgue, Valéry, Apollinaire, Supervielle, Éluard, Michaux and Desnos. English translations accompany the French originals. Notes appended to the volume place the poems in their historical and cultural context. Further discussions of the poetry included in this volume can be found in the editors' *Appreciation of modern French poetry (1850-1950)* (see next item).

428 **The appreciation of modern French poetry (1850-1950).**
Peter Broome, Graham Chesters. London, New York: Cambridge University Press, 1976. 166p. bibliog.
A companion volume to the editors' *Anthology of modern French poetry (1850-1950)* (previous item). The editors critically analyse two representative poems by each of the fourteen poets included in the anthology. In an introduction, the mechanics of French verse, from the 17th century Alexandrine to contemporary free form are discussed. A volume that can be highly recommended to anyone seeking to understand French poetry of the last one hundred years.

Contemporary

429 **Contemporary French literature, 1945 and after.**
Gaeton Picon, translated from the French by Kelvin W. Scott, Graham D. Martin. New York: F. Ungar, 1974. 227p. bibliog.
A straightforward history of thirty years of recent French literature by a well-known French critic who characterizes the contemporary era as a period of 'post-surrealism'. The book covers developments in fiction from the existentialists to the *nouveau roman* and textual writing, as well as new directions in poetry, the theatre, and literary criticism.

Literature. Contemporary

430 Modern French criticism from Proust and Valéry to structuralism.
Edited by John K. Simon. Chicago, Illinois: University of Chicago Press, 1972. 405p. bibliog.

It is sometimes difficult for the ordinary reader to follow French critics into the upper regions where they are apt to soar, but the authors of the essays collected in this volume have succeeded in making the abstractions with which French critics deal comprehensible. The book traces French literary criticism from the 1920s to the present, with essays devoted to the critical views of Valéry, Proust, Du Bos, Gourmont, Merleau-Ponty, the existentialists, the surrealists, the Geneva School, and the structuralists.

431 Contemporary French women poets: a bilingual critical anthology.
Edited and translated by Carl Hermey. San Francisco, California: Perivale Press, 207p. bibliog.

This anthology, which has received high praise from reviewers, contains the work of six contemporary women poets: Andrée Chedid, Annie Salager, Marie-Françoise Prager, Yvonne Caroutch, Denise Grappe, and Thérèse Plantier. The original poems and accompanying translations appear on facing pages. The book also contains a critical introduction and bibliographies.

432 The French novel from Gide to Camus.
Germaine Bree, Margaret Guiton. New York: Harcourt Brace Jovanovich, 1962. 241p. (Harbinger Book).

Bree, a well-known critic of French literature, views the novel of the first half of the 20th century as 'a reassertation of the inner reality of man', and defines its aim as an attempt 'to give individual life spiritual significance'. This book was first published in 1957 under the title *An age of fiction*; the 1962 paperback edition noted here adds a chapter on Beckett and the post-existentialist novel, in which Bree detects a shift away from humanistic interests towards concentration on literary and linguistic problems and technical sophistication.

433 *Chosisme*: a socio-psychological interpretation.
Zwedei Barbu. *European Journal of Sociology*, vol. 4, pt. 1 (1963), p. 127-47.

An illuminating discussion of the phenomenon of *chosisme* as exemplified in the novels of Robbe-Grillet. Barbu situates the *chosiste* novel in its psycho-social environment, and contrasts it with the psychological novel of the previous era. He points out the main features of the *chosiste* form: the predominance of the visual, the disappearance of the hero's interiority, and the blurring of sex roles, correlating these features with social changes and the disappearance of the bourgeois personality.

434 From Sartre to the new novel.
Betty T. Rahv. Port Washington, New York: Kennikat Press, 1974. 177p. bibliog. (National University Publication. Series in Literary Criticism).

Rahv sees Sartre's work as the starting point for the new paths taken by contemporary French fiction, and illustrates her thesis through discussions of Sartre's

Literature. Contemporary

'The childhood of a leader', Camus's *The stranger*, and Robbe-Grillet's *In the labyrinth*.

435 The French new novel: Claude Simon, Michel Butor, Alain Robbe-Grillet.
John Sturrock. London: Oxford University Press, 1969. 240p. bibliog.

Sturrock, a British critic, sees the *nouveau roman* as 'revolutionary in the best sense', and elucidates the innovations that the novel has undergone in the work of Simon, Butor, and Robbe-Grillet. In a similar work, *The nouveau roman; a study in the practice of writing* (Philadelphia, Pennyslvania: Temple University Press, 1972), Stephen Heath analyses the work of Sarraute, Robbe-Grillet, Simon, and Sollers.

436 The new novel from Queneau to Pinget.
Vivian Mercier. New York: Farrar, Straus, & Giroux, 1971. 425p. bibliog.

Mercier objects to the view that the *nouveau roman* was the literary embodiment of the philosophic movement of phenomenology. Rather, she holds, the new novel appeared as a response to the obsolescence of the novel of the first half of the 20th century, and was thus a purely literary phenomenon. The novelists whose work she considers representative of the movement are Queneau, Sarraute, Robbe-Grillet, Butor, Simon, Claude Mauriac, and Pinget.

437 French fiction today: a new direction.
Leon S. Roudiez. New Brunswick, New Jersey: Rutgers University Press, 1972. 413p. bibliog.

According to the author, the current generation of French writers has abandoned the humanism and concern for authenticity that obsessed their existentialist predecessors and are now 'attempting to break away from literature' through technique and linguistic effects. From this perspective, Roudiez discusses the work of Roussel, Sarraute, Blanchot, Beckett, Duras, Claude Mauriac, Simon, Pinget, Robbe-Grillet, Ollier, Saporta, Butor, Faye, Sollers, and Ricardou.

438 French novelists speak out.
Edited by Bettina Liebowitz Knapp. Troy, New York: Whitston Publishing Co., 1976. 177p.

A collection of interviews with French novelists, some well known - Michel Butor, Robert Pinget, Raymond Queneau, Francoise Mallet-Joris - others of lesser fame. A short biographical note identifying the writer precedes each interview. The interviews themselves are wide-ranging: the subjects discuss art, film, politics, and other topics besides their own work. The author states in her preface that 'the corpus of texts that follows offers a number of clues to the current state of French fiction'; readers with a bent for detection will enjoy this book.

Art

439 **Religious art in France: the twelfth century.**
Emile Mâle. Princeton, New Jersey: Princeton University Press, 1978. 575p. bibliog.
Reviewing this book in the *New York Times*, art critic John Russell called it 'a majestic volume' and a 'great work of scholarship' by 'an unsurpassed authority'. This edition is the first complete English translation of the 1922 French publication, a milestone in the history of art criticism in which Mâle established the right of the Romanesque style to be called 'great'.

440 **Art in medieval France, 987-1498.**
Joan Evans. London: Oxford University Press, 1948. 317p. bibliog.
A standard treatment of the art of the Middle Ages, by a well-known scholar and art historian. High-quality halftone illustrations add to the value of the book.

441 **French painting.**
R. H. Wilenski. London: Medici Society, 1949. Rev. ed. 310p.
A well-illustrated general account of French painting from the Middle Ages to the 20th century.

442 **Modern French painters.**
R. H. Wilenski. London: Faber, 1954. 3rd ed. 424p. bibliog.
A popular history of French painting, from the Impressionists to the Surrealists.

443 **An account of French painting.**
Clive Bell. London: Chatto & Windus, 1932. 219p.
A history of French painting by an influential British art critic.

Art

444 **The great wave: the influence of Japanese woodcuts on French prints.**
Colta Feller Ives. Boston, Massachusetts: New York Graphic Society, 1975. 116p. bibliog.

A book that discusses the influence of Ukiyo-e woodcuts on 19th century French etchings, woodcuts, and aquatints, in particular those of Gauguin and Toulouse-Lautrec.

445 **The absolute bourgeois: artists and politics in France, 1848-1851.**
T. J. Clark. Boston, Massachusetts: New York Graphic Society, 1973. 224p.

The author discusses the repercussions that social and political events had in the world of art in the tumultuous times following the Revolution of 1848. Particular attention is paid to the paintings of Daumier, Millet, and Delacroix, and to the poetry of Baudelaire.

446 **The history of Impressionism.**
John Rewald. Boston, Massachusetts: New York Graphic Society, 1973. 4th rev. ed. 672p. bibliog.

A complete chronicle of the Impressionist movement in France, splendidly illustrated with more than 600 plates. The book's value is further enhanced by an excellent critical bibliography.

447 **The Barbizon School and 19th-century French landscape painting.**
Jean Bouret. Boston, Massachusetts: New York Graphic Society, 1973. 271p. bibliog.

A basic study in English of the group of artists led by Théodore Rousseau who sought to paint from nature and dared to paint outdoors. This volume discusses the main adherents of the movement.

448 **Post-Impressionism: from Van Gogh to Gauguin.**
John Rewald. Boston, Massachusetts: New York Graphic Society, 1978. 3rd rev. ed. 584p. bibliog.

A standard work on the painters who succeeded the Impressionist movement in France. This revised edition contains new information and an updated bibliography.

449 **Dada, surrealism, and their heritage.**
William S. Rubin. Boston, Massachusetts: New York Graphic Society, 1968. 252p.

The Dadaists and the Surrealists represent two modern art movements especially identified with Paris. The philosophies behind these movements and the works they produced are amply and ably surveyed in this volume.

Art

450 **French decorative art, 1638-1793.**
George Savage. New York: Praeger, 1969. 188p. (Books That Matter).
A strikingly illustrated survey of the furniture, metalwork, small sculpture, ceramics, tapestry, and interior decoration of the classic centuries of French decor, from the reign of Louis XIV to that of Louis XVI.

451 **Seventeenth- and eighteenth-century French porcelain.**
George Savage. London, New York: Macmillan, 1960. 243p. bibliog.
One of the best introductions to the art of French porcelain available in English.

452 **French ceramics.**
Henri-Pierre Fourest. Tokyo, New York: Kodansha International, 1979. (Masterpieces of Western and Eastern Ceramics, 6).
An expensive but magnificent presentation of the ceramic art of France.

453 **French tapestry.**
Edited by Andre Lejard. London: Elek, 1946. 107p.
A collection of articles on the history and technique of French tapestry. Well illustrated.

454 **The French garden, 1500-1800.**
William H. Adams. New York: Braziller, 1979. 160p. (World Landscape Art and Architecture series).
Covers evolution of the French garden over a 300 year period. Another interesting monograph on the French garden is *The French formal garden*, edited by Elizabeth B. MacDougall and F. Hamilton Hazelhurst (Washington, D.C., 1974).

Architecture and City Planning

455 **Architecture of France.**
Bruce Allsopp, Ursula Clark. London: Oriel Press, 1963. 96p.

A handy guidebook. A concise overview of the history of buildings down to the present, with the last four pages devoted to vernacular architecture. A final section lists touring routes 'devised so that each one gives an opportunity to study a particular sort of architecture'. This book is an excellent vade mecum for travellers with a special interest in architecture.

456 **A history of architecture in France.**
T. W. West. London: University of London Press, 1969. 232p. bibliog.

A survey that confines itself to representative works, focusing 'only on those buildings which illustrate an evolutionary theme - particularly the first appearances of new forms and styles - or are outstanding in themselves'.

457 **A history of French architecture.**
Reginald Blomfield. London: G. Bell & Sons, 1911-21. 4 vols. Reprinted, New York: Hacker Art Books, 1974.

This was once the authoritative work for French architecture from the reign of Charles VIII to the death of Louis XV (1494-1774). Although now superseded by later scholarship, these volumes retain their interest, and architectural libraries that do not own the original edition will wish to purchase the reprint.

Architecture and City Planning

458 **Three hundred years of French architecture, 1494-1794.**
Reginald Blomfield. New York: Macmillan, 1936. 129p.
Reprinted, New York: Arno, 1975.
The author states in his preface that this is 'a short introduction addressed to the general reader indicating the main lines of development of [the] movement of French Neo-classic architecture'.

459 **Gothic architecture.**
Louis Grodecki, in collaboration with Anne Prache, Roland Recht, translated from the French by I. Mark. Paris: Abrams, 1977. 442p. bibliog. (History of World Architecture series).
A well-illustrated synthesis of what is known about Gothic architecture. Deals with 12th and 13th century French architecture in the context of the total European development of the style.

460 **French cathedrals.**
Martin Hurlimann, Jean Bony. New York: Viking Press, 1967. New rev. ed. 229p. (Studio Book).
A large volume whose photographs capture the majesty and drama of the great cathedrals of France.

461 **Gothic cathedrals of France.**
Marcel Aubert, in collaboration with Simone Goubet, translated from the French by L. Kochan, M. Kochan, assisted by George Millard. London: Nicholas Kaye, 1959. 170p.
Exhaustive descriptions of the French cathedrals accompany 462 detailed photographs of the churches and of the art and sculpture of their interiors.

462 **Monastic architecture in France from the Renaissance to the Revolution.**
Joan Evans. London: Cambridge University Press, 1964. 186p. bibliog.
The standard work in English on the architecture of the French religious orders. Illustrated with 800 plates.

463 **The architecture of the Renaissance in France: a history of the evolution of the arts of building, decoration and garden design under classical influence from 1495 to 1830.**
W. H. Ward. New York: Scribner's, 1926. 2nd ed., rev., 2 vols. bibliog. Reprinted, New York: Hacker Art Books, 1976. 533p.
An old, but basic work on French Renaissance architecture, recently reprinted.

Architecture and City Planning

464 **New French architecture.**
Maurice Besset. New York: Praeger, 1967. 235p. (Books That Matter).
A survey of modern architecture in France, from the end of the Second World War to the 1960s. Thickly illustrated with photographs. Text in French and English.

465 **France.**
Haig Beck. New York: Rizzoli International Publications, 1979. 104p. (AD profiles).
A paperback volume that covers the last ten years of French architecture in 200 illustrations.

466 **The French new towns.**
James M. Rubenstein. Baltimore, Maryland: Johns Hopkins University Press, 1978. 192p. maps.
Nine new towns are currently under construction in France. Rubenstein's book - the most complete treatment yet published of French ventures into town planning - is a case study of their development, examining the administrative, financial and political obstacles faced by French planners and describing how these obstacles were surmounted.

467 **Urban development in Western Europe: France and Belgium.**
Edwin Gutkind. New York: Free Press, 1979. 544p. maps. bibliog. (International History of City Development, 5).
The most complete study in English of the development of French cities. Profusely illustrated with photographs, maps, and diagrams.

Music and Dance

468 **French music in the fifteenth and sixteenth centuries.**
Isabelle Cazeaux. New York: Praeger, 1975. 312p. bibliog.
This is not a chronological history of French music, but rather a volume that studies the place of music in the social and cultural life of the French Renaissance. As such, social historians as well as musicologists will find it of interest. Covers music in the royal courts and in aristocratic and ecclesiastical circles; music written for personal and political occasions; the influence of music on language, mores, morals, and education; music in contests, the theatre, on the road and in the street; music in the cemetery, the field, and the hunt; and military music.

469 **French opera: its development to the Revolution.**
Norman Demuth. Horsham, England: Artemis Press, 1963. 337p. bibliog.
The author states in his foreword that his book is an attempt to fill a gap in the literature on French music in English: he has taken up his subject because he had tried in vain to find an English book dealing exclusively with French opera and opera in France. The work traces French opera from its origins in the liturgical drama of the Middle Ages to the Revolution, with the major part of the book devoted to Lully. Many details of the social history of music are included in the presentation.

470 **French grand opera: an art and a business.**
William L. Crosten. New York: King's Crown Press, 1948. 162p. bibliog. Reprinted, New York: Da Capo, 1972.
Originally a thesis presented for a degree at Columbia University, this book is a study of French grand opera of the 1830s when Meyerbeer and his associates enjoyed a 'fabulous success'. The author has written a comprehensive study of this musical phenomenon, at the same time a commercial success and an ambitious art form which 'attempted to give a new large-scale design to opera'. He also considers French grand opera as a social document and finds that its implications illuminate French society in the era following the Revolution of 1830.

Music and Dance

471 **Modern French music.**
Edward Burlingame Hill. New York: Houghton Mifflin, 1924. 406p. bibliog. Reprinted, New York: Da Capo, 1969.

An older book, which charts the course of French music from the Franco-Prussian War to the 1920s. Although somewhat old-fashioned in its critical approach - it 'regards the music of each composer as the spontaneous reaction of his temperament upon his environment' - general readers may find it useful. The presentation is nontechnical and the author provides information about the lesser-known as well as the celebrated composers of the period. Among those included are Henri Rabaud, Gabriel Fauré, Erik Satie, Vincent d'Indy, Joseph-Marie-Guy Ropartz, Claude Debussy, Maurice Ravel, and Albert Roussel.

472 **French music: from the death of Berlioz to the death of Fauré.**
Martin Cooper. London, New York: Oxford University Press, 1951. Reprinted, 1969. 239p. bibliog.

A book written expressly to explain the course of French music from 1869 to 1924 to the English public. The author notes that 'music has remained in France longer than elsewhere the art of arranging sounds in agreeable and intellectually satisfying patterns', the French viewing a piece of music 'as an artefact - rather than as the expression of an emotion whose end is itself'.

473 **Modern French music: from Fauré to Boulez.**
Rollo Myers. New York: Praeger, 1971. 210p. bibliog.

Traces the history of French music from 1900 to 1969. The author comments that for much of this period France held first place in the music world: 'from 1900 to the beginning of the Second World War, France, more than any other country, represented all that was best and most vital in twentieth-century music'. During these forty years, 'French music and modern music were synonymous'. Myers gives the background and events of the period and discusses the work of the leading composers Fauré, Debussy, Ravel, Satie, 'Les Six', Varese, and Messiaen among them. The final section of the volume deals with developments in 20th century opera, ballet, and choral music.

474 **French music since Debussy and Ravel.**
Royal S. Brown. *High Fidelity*, vol. 23 (Sept. 1973), p. 50-65.

A compact survey of the past fifty years of French music, from 'Les Six' to *musique concrète*. Includes lists of recommended recordings of the music discussed in the article.

475 **Dances of England and France from 1450-1600: with their music and authentic manner of performance.**
Mabel Dolmetsch. London: Routledge & Kegan Paul, 1949. 163p. bibliog. Reprinted, New York: Da Capo, 1975.

This is not a history of the dance; rather, it is a book that describes and gives instructions and music for the performance of such Renaissance dances as the *basse* dance, the *branle*, the *pavan*, and the *galliard*. The work is based on original manuscript materials.

Music and Dance

476 The ballet of the Second Empire.
Ivor Guest. London: Pitman; Middleton, Connecticut: Wesleyan University Press, 1974. 279p. bibliog.

Although at first glance this study of ballet in the Paris of Napoleon III seems a somewhat specialized volume, the general reader should not be deterred, as he will find much to interest him. The author's aim is 'to chronicle the events of the ballet and bring to life some of the people involved in it against the setting of the period...believing that the history of an art form is inseparable from contemporary trends in thought and the social and political conditions of the time'.

Theatre and Film

477 **French tragic drama in the sixteenth and seventeenth centuries.**
Geoffrey Brereton. London: Methuen; New York: Barnes & Noble, 1973. 312p. bibliog. (University Paperbacks, 498).
In an excellent account of a central period of French literature, the author succinctly presents the drama in France as it developed from the mediaeval *mystères* (outlawed in 1548) to the late 17th century tragedies of Racine.

478 **An introduction to the French theatre.**
Peter D. Arnott. Totowa, New Jersey: Rowman & Littlefield, 1977. 164p. bibliog.
Although this book includes a rapid survey of the history of the French theatre from the Middle Ages to the Renaissance, and makes some comments on the modern theatre, its emphasis is on the 17th century theatre of Racine and Molière.

479 **The Theatre in Dada and Surrealism.**
J. H. Matthews. Syracuse, New York: Syracuse University Press, 1974. 286p.
A detailed and sympathetic treatment of an important period of the 20th century theatre that has not received the attention it deserves. The author studies the work of fifteen Dadaists and Surrealists.

480 **Modern French theatre from Giraudoux to Genet.**
Jacques Guicharnaud, in collaboration with June Guicharnaud. New Haven, Connecticut: Yale University Press, 1967. 383p. bibliog.
The challenging theatre produced by French playwrights of the past fifty years is analysed in this stimulating study which discusses the works of Giraudoux, Cocteau, Claudel, Salacrou, Montherlant, Anouilh, Sartre, Camus, Arrabal, Adamov, Ionesco, Beckett, and Genet. Appendices list directors and productions and first performances and important revivals of modern plays.

Theatre and Film

481 **The French cinema since 1946.**
Roy Armes. Cranbury, New Jersey: A. S. Barnes, 1970.
2nd enlarged ed. 2 vols.
An analysis and history of postwar films. Volume 1 is entitled 'The great tradition', volume 2 'The personal style'.

482 **French film.**
Georges Sadoul. London: Falcon Press, 1953. 131p.
Reprinted, New York: Arno, 1972. (Literature of the
Cinema series).
A history of the motion picture in France, from its earliest days to the postwar era.

483 **The new wave: Truffaut, Godard, Chabrol, Rohmer, Rivette.**
James Monaco. New York: Oxford University Press, 1977.
372p. bibliog.
A critical study of the work of the five directors who reoriented the French cinema.

Publishing and the Press

484 **Publishing in France.**
Herbert R. Lottman. *Publishers Weekly*, vol. 215, pt. 18 (30 April 1979), p. 53-102.
A lengthy report on publishing in France that covers the book market, publishing rights, textbook publishing, book clubs, major French publishers, new publishers, and English language bookstores in Paris.

485 **Cercle de la Librairie: a model book trade organization.**
Herbert R. Lottman. *Publishers Weekly*, vol. 207 (3 March 1975), p. 35-6.
A two-page article on the Cercle de la Librairie, the trade association of French publishing, and the Syndicat National de l'Edition, the French book publishers' organization. The article describes the services that these organizations direct for the book trade and the bookbuying public from their headquarters at 117 Boulevard St. Germain.

486 **The history makers: the press of Europe from its beginnings through 1965.**
Kenneth E. Olson. Baton Rouge, Louisiana: Louisiana State University Press, 1966. 471p. bibliog.
A chapter entitled 'The individualistic Gallic press' gives a short history of the French press from its beginnings in 1695 with the *Mercure de France* to the 1960s, and explains the organization of the contemporary French press. A short bibliography lists French and English sources on the French press.

Publishing and the Press

487 **The *Paris Herald*: the incredible newspaper.**
Al Laney. New York: D. Appleton-Century, 1947. 334p.
Reprinted, New York: Greenwood Press, 1968.
A sprightly, anecdotal account of the *Paris Herald*, from its founding in 1887 to the Second World War.

Newspapers, Magazines, and Periodicals

Dailies

488 L'Aurore.
Paris.
L'Aurore is a daily newspaper which represents conservative opinion in France and has national distribution. Between 1972 and 1977 its readership declined by one-third.

489 La Croix.
Paris.
The Catholic daily newspaper, written from a liberal Catholic viewpoint. Its circulation is approximately 126,500 copies.

490 L'Est Republicain.
Nancy.
A morning provincial daily with a circulation of close to half a million copies.

491 Le Figaro.
Paris.
This Parisian daily represents the views of the moderate right. Its readership has dropped slightly over the past seven years, but its weekly, *Le Figaro Littéraire*, has the largest printing of the literary French weeklies.

Newspapers, Magazines, and Periodicals. Dailies

492 France-Soir.
Paris.
The evening daily paper of Paris. Its circulation has declined sharply in the past few years, from over a million copies to around 727,000 copies - still, however, an impressive figure in a country where only twenty-seven out of every hundred inhabitants read a daily newspaper.

493 L'Humanité.
Paris.
The daily newspaper of the French Communist Party, with a circulation of around 161,000 copies. Its Sunday edition, *L'Humanité-Dimanche*, has a circulation of over 400,000 copies.

494 International Herald Tribune.
Paris.
The American-managed, English-language daily morning paper, with a circulation of around 177,000 copies.

495 Le Monde.
Paris.
Le Monde enjoys an international reputation for its superior journalism. Its articles are lengthy, detailed, and intellectually demanding, and it follows a policy of not printing photographs. Has a circulation of around 290,000 copies.

496 Le Nouveau Journal.
Paris.
A financial newspaper, with a circulation of 59,000 copies; a second financial and economic newspaper, also published in Paris, is *Les Échos*, which has a circulation of 53,814 copies.

497 Ouest-France.
Rennes.
The leading provincial daily morning paper, with a circulation of slightly less than one million copies.

498 Le Parisien-Libéré.
Paris.
Le Parisien-Libéré competes with *France-Soir* for leadership of the popular press. Its circulation is close to 786,000 copies.

499 Le Progrès.
Lyons.
A regional daily paper. As has been the case with most French newspapers, its circulation has declined in recent years.

Newspapers, Magazines, and Periodicals.
Weeklies, monthlies, etc.

500 **Le Provençal.**
Marseilles.
The daily newspaper of Marseilles, with wide distribution in Southeast France. The editorial outlook is socialist. *Le Provençal* is one of the few French newspapers whose readership has increased, rather than declined, in recent years: it now has a circulation of approximately 379,000 copies.

501 **La Voix du Nord.**
Lille.
A daily morning newspaper with a circulation of about 382,000 copies.

Weeklies, monthlies, etc.

502 **Le Canard Enchaîné: journal satirique paraissant le mercredi.** (The Chained Duck: a satirical newspaper appearing every Wednesday.)
Paris: Éditions Marechal, 1915-, weekly.
The well-known satirical weekly that practises an amusing if sometimes startling brand of political satire, with its numerous cartoons calculated to offend the government. Has a large circulation of 450,000 copies.

503 **Critique.**
Paris: Les Editions de Minuit, 1946-, monthly.
Critique reviews four to ten books a month in detailed and intellectually demanding articles. Among its regular features is a 'notes' section on the current French literary scene.

504 **Écrits de Paris: revue des questions actuelles.** (Writings from Paris: a review of current events.)
Paris: Société Parisienne d'Éditions et de Publication, 1945-, monthly.
A well-written conservative publication that focuses on controversial current events. Its regular columns discuss books and culture.

505 **Elle.** (She.)
Paris, 1945-, weekly.
A popular magazine that competes with *Marie-France* (q.v.) for the woman reader. Published every Monday, *Elle* has a circulation of 600,000 copies.

Newspapers, Magazines, and Periodicals.
Weeklies, monthlies, etc.

506 **Esprit.** (Spirit.)
Paris: Editions Esprit SARL, 1932-, monthly.

The magazine of the Catholic avant-garde, founded in 1932 by Emmanuel Mounier and currently edited by Jean-Marie Domenach. Its articles of social and literary criticism are written from a liberal Catholic viewpoint.

507 **L'Express.** (Express.)
Paris: Express, 1957-, weekly.

The leading French news magazine, *L'Express* appears in a format similar to the American *Time*, but takes a slightly more intellectual approach to current events. Its political viewpoint is liberal, and it has a circulation of approximately 600,000 copies.

508 **Film Français.** (French film.)
Paris, 1918-, weekly.

A weekly presentation of the news of the French and European film and television worlds.

509 **Le Français dans le Monde.** (French in the World.)
Paris: Hachette & Larousse, 1961-, 8 times per year.

This respected publication for teachers of French includes both scholarship and practical articles.

510 **Historia.**
Paris, 1946-, monthly.

A magazine of popular history whose large circulation - over 320,000 copies - testifies to the appeal this subject holds for the general French public.

511 **Marie-France.**
Paris, 1944-, monthly.

A popular women's magazine that emphasizes middle-class fashions, home decorating, cooking, and entertainment. Circulation of around 660,000 copies.

512 **Paris Match.**
Paris: Union de Publications et d'Editions Modernes, 1949-, weekly.

Paris Match is aimed at the middle- and lower-middle-class reader; photographs of French celebrities and events dominate its issues.

513 **Le Nouvel Observateur.** (The New Observer.)
Paris, 1964-, weekly.

French news and contemporary French culture presented and commented on from a leftist viewpoint. Contains book, film, music, and drama reviews.

Newspapers, Magazines, and Periodicals.
Weeklies, monthlies, etc.

514 **Nouvelle Revue Française.** (New French Review.)
Paris: Gallimard, 1953-, monthly.

The successor to the renowned *NRF*, founded in 1908, that ceased publication in 1943. The editor of the *Nouvelle Revue Fraçaise* is Marcel Arland; the periodical presents serious articles on literature, film, theatre, music and art.

515 **Nouvelles Littéraires; arts, sciences, spectacles.** (Literary News; arts, sciences, entertainment.)
Paris, 1922-, weekly.

A tabloid newspaper that features news of French culture; its regular departments cover science, education, and the social sciences. Reviews radio and television programmes as well as books and films.

516 **Officiel de la Couture et de la Mode de Paris.** (The Gazette of Paris Fashion and Dressmaking.)
Paris, 1921-, 10 times per year.

The magazine of Paris fashion. Each issue contains from two to three hundred pages of photographs of current Paris collections. Text in French with English, German, and Spanish translations.

517 **Le Quinzaine Littéraire.** (The Literary Fortnightly.)
Paris, 1966-, bimonthly.

Each issue of this thirty-page tabloid contains a few brief articles and many book reviews.

518 **Revue Historique.** (Historical Review.)
Paris: Presses Universitaires de France, 1876-, quarterly.

Edited at present by two noted French historians, Jean Favier and René Remond, this quarterly is the major French periodical in the field of historical scholarship. Excellent bibliographical articles often appear in this publication.

519 **Tel Quel: littérature-philosophie-science-politique.** (As It Is: literature-philosophy-science-politics.)
Paris: Éditions du Seuil, 1960-, quarterly.

A recent addition to the list of French literary-social reviews, *Tel Quel* is a scholarly journal with a Marxist viewpoint. Its current editor is Marcelin Pleynet.

520 **Les Temps Modernes.** (Modern Times.)
Paris, 1945-, monthly.

A highly intellectual social-political review, founded and still directed by Jean-Paul Sartre.

Newspapers, Magazines, and Periodicals.
Outside France.

Periodicals published outside France

521 **France Education.**
New York: French Embassy Cultural Services, 1974-, irregular.
Formerly entitled *French News*, this brief publication is designed to aid the secondary school teacher of French. Each issue is written in French, and contains articles on education and on French culture.

522 **French Historical Studies.**
Columbus, Ohio: Society for French Historical Studies, 1958-, semi-annual.
A scholarly journal that publishes four to six articles per issue on French history. At the end of each issue there appears a list of 'Recent books on French history'.

523 **French Review.**
Chapel Hill, North Carolina: American Association of Teachers of French, 1927-
Directed at the teacher of French at the college or secondary school level, this magazine contains articles on literature, history and language. It also publishes professional notes, reports on dissertations in progress, and reviews of books of interest to teachers.

524 **French Studies.**
Belfast, North Ireland: Society for French Studies, 1947-, quarterly.
An academic journal, sponsored by the Department of French of the Queen's University of Belfast, that publishes scholarly articles on French literature. Each issue of the periodical also contains many book reviews.

525 **Yale French Studies.**
New Haven, Connecticut: Yale University Dept. of French, 1948-, semi-annual.
A scholarly journal that publishes intellectually demanding articles on French culture. Each issue is organized around one topic.

Encyclopaedias and Directories

526 **La grande encyclopédie.** (The great encyclopaedia.)
Paris: Larousse, 1972-76. 21 vols. maps.
A standard reference work, entries arranged alphabetically. Very good on science and technology. Another subject encyclopaedia that can be recommended is the *Bordas encyclopédie* (Paris, 1971-75) in 23 vols.

527 **Quid 1978.**
Paris: Robert Laffont, 1978. 1488p.
A wide-ranging one-volume mini-encyclopaedia packed with information about France. Revised each year, *Quid* provides facts, dates, and statistics on every aspect of French life: architecture, literature, music, celebrities, actors, cinema, theatre, politics, transport, tourism, education, national defence, money and prices, the stock market, banks and credit associations, the press, radio and television, business enterprises, and commerce. Each region and department of the country is described in detail, with the facts of its history, geography, climate, resources, economic activities, population, and tourist attractions noted.

528 **Qui est qui en France, 1977-1978.** (Who's who in France, 1977-78.)
Paris: Editions Jacques Lafitte, 1977. 13th ed. 1680p.
The *Who's Who* of France has been published every two years since 1953. The 1977-78 edition contains 22,000 biographical entries for living Frenchmen and Frenchwomen, as well as for foreigners residing in France. The volume also includes directory information on national enterprises, research institutes, professional associations, financial institutions, insurance companies, banks, and businesses.

Encyclopaedias and Directories

529 **Bottin administratif et documentaire.**
Paris: Société Didot Bottin, annual.
The official directory of the French government and administration. Besides listing government officials, the publication includes a table of the constitutions of France since 1789 and the text of the constitution of the Fifth Republic, as well as statistics and helpful information on law, weights and measures, transport and communications, military service, and civil matters.

Museums, Archives and Libraries

530 **Trésors des musées de province.** (Treasures of provincial museums.)
Georges Merz, Edmond Prouverelle (and others). Paris: Société d'Éditions de la Revue française, 1957-61. 4 vols.
A detailed and comprehensive guide to the collections of provincial art museums.

531 **Répertoire des musées de France et de la Communauté.** (Directory of museums in France and in the Community.) G. Barnaud. Paris: Institut Pédagogique National, 1959. 416p.
A directory of all types of museums. Arranged alphabetically by names of towns. Entries give information on curators, hours, and the nature of the collections.

532 **The new guide to the diplomatic archives of Western Europe.**
Edited by Daniel H. Thomas, Lynn M. Case. Philadelphia, Pennsylvania: University of Pennsylvania Press, 1975. 441p. bibliog.
An expanded and updated version of the editors' 1959 *Guide to the diplomatic archives of Western Europe*. Chapter 5, 'France' by Vincent Confer, covers the Archives du Ministère des Affaires Etrangères at 37 Quai d'Orsay, explaining the history, organization, and classification of the collection, and describing its administration, regulations, and the facilities available to scholars. A bibliography of printed collections of documents, guides, and reference works pertaining to these archives is appended to the chapter.

Museums, Archives and Libraries

533 **Les archives de l'histoire de France: manuels de bibliographie historique.** (Archives of French history: handbooks of historical bibliography.)
Charles V. Langlois, Henri Stein. Paris: A. Picard, 1891. 1,000p. Reprinted, Nendeln, Liechtenstein: Kraus, 1966.

The standard guide to French and overseas archives and records. For the National Archives, it is supplemented by C. Schmidt's *Sources de l'histoire de France depuis 1789 aux Archives Nationales* (1907).

534 **État des inventaires des archives nationales, départementales, communales et hospitalières, au 1er janvier 1937.** (A list of the inventories of national, departmental, communal, and hospital archives, as of 1 January 1937.)
H. Courteault (for the Direction des Archives de France). Paris: Didier, 1938. 703p. bibliog.

Lists and describes inventories of several types of French archives. A *Supplément, 1937-1954* was compiled by Robert H. Boutier.

535 **Répertoire des bibliothèques et organismes de documentation.** (Directory of libraries and documentation centres.)
Bibliothèque Nationale. Paris: Bibliothèque Nationale, 1971. 4th ed. 3 vols. in 1.

The official directory of French libraries: the 1971 edition is the fourth published in thirty years, updating the third edition of 1963. It lists 3,210 libraries and documentation centres, 1,315 in the Paris region and the remaining 1,895 in the other departments and overseas territories of France. The address, regulations, catalogues, and resources of each library are given. The book includes subject and name indexes.

536 **Libraries in Paris: a student's guide.**
L. M. Newman. Scorton, Lancashire, England: Conder Research, 1971. 175p. bibliog. (Conder Library and Information Studies, 1).

A practical guide, designed to give the English-speaking student in the humanities, who is approaching the libraries of Paris for the first time, the benefit of the author's experience. Describes the libraries - national, university, municipal, special, private, and archival - in detail. Includes model letters for those seeking entry to Parisian collections and a directory of Paris libraries and documentation centres, as well as helpful sections on research tools and French library terminology.

537 **Libraries in France.**
John Ferguson. Hamden, Connecticut: Archon, 1971. 120p. bibliog. (Comparative Library Studies).

A short description of the library situation in France in 1970. Ferguson's survey covers the entire country in a narrative account. The book begins with a description of the government bureau which administers French libraries, the *Direction des bibliothèques et de la lecture publique*, then discusses the many types of

Museums, Archives and Libraries

libraries that constitute the French library system: national, Parisian, public and municipal, school and children's, rural, and university. Other topics covered are library methodology, interlibrary cooperation, the library profession, the education of librarians, and professional library associations.

538 **The current French library scene.**
Richard K. Gardner. *Wilson Library Bulletin*, vol. 43, pt. 10 (June 1969), p. 982-91.

A short article describing the changes projected for French libraries as a result of the events of May-June 1968. The author begins with an account of the centralized administrative structure of the French library system, then summarizes the progress made in the organization of a network of regional lending libraries since the Second World War; he discusses the expansion and renovation of the Parisian municipal library system, new ideas for school libraries and library education, and concludes by noting recent efforts at improving, coordinating and rebudgeting library services in France.

Bibliographies

539 **La bibliographie de la France: journal officiel du livre français.** (The bibliography of France: official gazette of the French book trade.)
Paris: Cercle de la Librairie, 1812-
This is a *grande dame* of national bibliographies, having been created by imperial decree in 1812. It is the official weekly record of French book publishing, its listings being based on copyright submissions to the Bibliothèque Nationale. Besides the weekly issues, subscribers receive a monthly summary of the weekly listings, *Livres du Mois*; a quarterly cumulation, *Tables Trimestrielles des Nouveautés*; and a yearly bound volume, *Les Livres de l'Année-Biblio*, of over 25,000 titles - the worldwide output of French-language publishing. Special supplements reviewing the bibliography of particular topics and special catalogues of gift and school books are also part of the bibliography.

540 **How to find out about France: a guide to sources of information.**
John E. Pemberton. New York: Pergamon Press, 1966. 199p.
The most recent guide in English to survey the entire range of literature devoted to France. Titles are presented in a narrative, with brief comments and without full bibliographical details. As most of the works noted are in French, the user is presupposed to have a reading knowledge of the language. The book is divided into chapters, each dealing with a subject field or a type of publication: national bibliographies and encyclopedias; philosophy and religion; government, society and the press; industry and commerce; the language; dictionaries; science and technology; art and architecture; music; theatre, drama, cinema; literary history; literature; poetry; prose fiction; geography and travel; and archaeology, biography and history. The book is valuable, not only for the many titles covered, but for its reliable listing of the standard French works and comprehensive French treatises in many subject fields.

Bibliographies

541 **French Periodical Index.**
Compiled by Jean-Pierre Ponchie. Westwood, Massachusetts: F. W. Faxon Co., 1976-, annual. (Useful Reference Series).

This subject index to articles in contemporary French-language periodicals was begun in 1976, with the first volume covering 1973-74. In 1977 the index went into computerized production and volumes for 1975 and 1976 were published. In 1978, a volume for 1977 was produced. The list of periodicals indexed has varied slightly since the first volume. The periodicals chosen for inclusion in the 1977 volume were *L'Actualité, Les Dossiers et Documents du Monde, L'Express, Le Français dans le Monde, Jeune Afrique, Le Monde de l'Éducation, Le Monde Hebdomadaire, Le Nouvel Observateur, Paris-Match*, and *Réalités*.

542 **An annotated bibliography of French language and literature.**
Fernande Bassan, Paul F. Breed, Donald C. Spinelli. New York, London: Garland Publishing Co., 1976. 306p. (Garland Reference Library of the Humanities, 26).

In spite of its literary slant, this bibliography should prove valuable to those researching other aspects of French life and culture, as the first section of the volume covers general bibliographical and research tools in much detail. The second part of the volume lists works on French language, and the third section, works on French literature and 'selective studies on history, civilization, philosophy, and religion'. The last chapter covers the literature of French expression in countries other than France.

Index

The index is a single alphabetical sequence of authors (personal and corporate), titles of publications and subjects. Index entries refer both to the main items and to other works mentioned in the notes to each item. Title entries are in italics. Numeration refers to the items as numbered.

A

Abbreviations, Scientific 407
Abbreviations, Technological 407
Absolute bourgeois: artists and politics in France, 1848-1851 445
Absolutism 72−73, 76
Account of French painting 443
Acomb, E. M. 83
Action Française 119, 121, 266, 268−270
Action Française: die-hard reactionaries in twentieth-century France 269
Action Française: royalism and reaction in twentieth-century France 268
Adamov, Arthur 480
Adams, W. H. 454
Administration 18−19, 312
 directories 529
 Third Republic 320
Administration and technocracy 311
Administrative courts 307−308, 321
Administrative functions of the French Conseil d'État 308
Administrative law 326
Administrators 313−317
 local 322−323

Adrienne 406
Aerial photographs 26
Aerospace industries 394
Aesthetic thought of the French Enlightenment 175
Aesthetics
 18th century 175−176
Affluence and the French worker in the Fourth Republic 264
Africa
 French possessions 152−153, 155
 African member states 296
 post-colonial relations 330
Afrique noire 155
Age of Charlemagne 60
Age of fiction, An 432
Aged, The 214−215
Agricultural productivity and economic development in France, 1852-1950, with the revised French version 372
Agriculture 20, 371, 373
 19th century 345, 372
 20th century 203, 208, 345, 372
 development 10
 EEC policy 292
 history 370, 372
 statistics 250, 253

145

Air pollution 381
Alcohol and alcoholism 216
Algeria
  20th century 141
  history 141
  insurrection, 1954-62 138—141, 165
Algerian immigrants 236, 244—246
Algerian insurrection, 1954-1962 138
Algerian problem 140
Alhadeff, D. 350
Alleman, F. R. 241
Allsopp, B. 455
Alsatians, The 235, 241—242
Altbach, Philip G. 233
Aluminium industries 353
Ambiguous consensus: a study of local government in France 322
Ambler, J. S. 265, 304
America and French culture, 1750-1848 290
American and French culture, 1800-1900: interchanges in art, science, literature and society 291
American Association of Teachers of French 523
American challenge 198
Ancien Régime 86—87
Anderson, B. G. 207
Anderson, Frank Maloy 328
Anderson, G. 243
Anderson, M. 242, 267, 306
Anderson, R. 202, 243
Anderson, R. D. 118
Anderson, R. T. 207
Angoumois
  folklore 159
Animal literature, Mediaeval 413
Annales school 370
Annales school of historiography 187, 194
Annotated bibliography of French language and literature 542
Anouilh, Jean 480
Anthology of modern French poetry 427
Anthropology
  20th century 184
  economic 184
Anti-philosophers: a study of the philosophes in eighteenth-century France 173
Anti-Semitism 248—249
Anti-Semitism in modern France 249
Anticlericalism
  19th century 107

Apolitisme 322
Apollinaire, Guillaume 425, 427
Appreciation of modern French poetry 428
Aqueducts 397
Arabs
  French administration in Morocco 154
Archaeology 42, 44
  bibliographies 540
  research 43
Architecture 50
  12th century 459, 461
  13th century 459, 461
  15th century 462
  16th century 457—458, 462—463
  17th century 457—458, 462—463
  18th century 457—458, 462—463
  20th century 52, 464—465
  bibliographies 540
  Carolingian 60
  cathedrals 460
  Gallo-Roman 52
  Gothic 459, 461
  history 455—459, 461—465
  Neo-Classical 457—458
  Renaissance 463
  tours 455
Architecture, Monastic 462
Architecture of France 455
Architecture of the Renaissance in France: a history of the evolution of the arts of building, decoration and garden design under classical influence from 1495 to 1830 463
Architecture, Religious 460—461
Archives 533—534
  directories 536
  Paris 536
Archives, Departmental 534
Archives, Diplomatic 532
Archives, National 533—534
Arcueil, Society of 391
Ardagh, J. 10
Arguments group 200
Arland, Marcel 514
Armagnac 386
Armes, R. 481
Armorica 42
Armstrong, J. A. 313
Army 50
  17th century 75
  20th century 265
  political attitudes 265

Arnott, P. D. 478
Aron, R. 129
Aron, Raymond 2, 195, 299
Arrabal, Fernando 480
Art 5—6, 438, 441—444, 446—453
  11th century 440
  12th century 440
  13th century 440
  14th century 440
  15th century 440
  16th century 69
  19th century 445
  Basque 156
  bibliographies 540
  Carolingian 60
  folk 160
  Gallo-Roman 52—53
  history 440, 445
  periodicals 514
  religious 165, 439
Art and society 445
Art, Decorative 50, 463
  17th century 450
  18th century 450
  history 450
Art galleries 41
  directories 530
Art in medieval France, 987-1498 440
As France goes 7
Aspects of French Jewry: studies 247
Assemblée des Notables 87
Assignment to catastrophe 125
Atkinson, J. B. 48
Atlas historique de la France contemporaine, 1800-1965 36
Atlas historique et culturel de la France 37
Atlases
  bibliographies 20
Atlases and maps 32—37
Atmospheric pollution 381
Atomic energy policy in France under the Fourth Republic 297
Atomic weapons 297—298
Attack on 'feudalism' in eighteenth-century France 178
Aubert, M. 461
Aulard, François Alphonse 98
Automata
  18th century 395
Automobile industries 353, 359
Autopsie de la guerre d'Algérie 140
Autoroute de l'Est 374
Aviation industries 375, 394
Avril, P. 257

B

Bagnolet, Paris 215
Baguettes 389
Bailyn, Bernard 187
Balance of payments 341
Ballet
  19th century 476
  20th century 473
  history 476
Ballet of the Second Empire 476
Balloons
  18th century 395
Balzac, Honoré de 46, 419, 422
Bandyopadhyay, P. 189
Banine 236
Banks and banking 350—351
Banque de France 351
Banville, Théodore de 424
Barbarism with a human face 190
Barber, E. G. 85
Barber, M. 184
Barber, N. 124
Barbizon school 447
Barbizon School and 19th-century French landscape painting 447
Barbu, Z. 433
Barère de Vieuzac, Bertrand 100
Barnard, H. C. 221
Barnaud, G. 531
Barrès, Maurice 119
Barthes, R. 9
Basque
  language and literature 156
Basques 239
Basques, The 202, 235, 237—239
  culture 156
  folklore 156
  history 156
Bassan, F. 542
Batteux, Charles 175
Bauchet, P. 338
Baudelaire, Charles 421, 427, 445
Baum, W. C. 335
Bayle, Pierre 170
Beaujeu-Garnier, J. 22
Beck, H. 465
Beckett, Samuel 437, 480
Beer, S. H. 256
Beer, W. R. 58
Behr, E. 140
Bell, C. 443
Beloff, N. 293

147

Ben-David, J. 396
Benguigui, G. 247
Berbers
　French administration in
　　Morocco 154
Berger, Suzanne 205, 256, 262
Bernanos, Georges 194
Bernard, Claude 398
Bernard, Stéphane 154
Besset, M. 464
Bestiaries 413
Between center and periphery: grassroots politicians in Italy and France 323
Biblio 539
La bibliographie de la France: journal officiel du livre français 539
Bibliographies 540
　17th century 76
　19th century 426
　20th century 426
　civilization 542
　colonialism 152
　Consulat, 1799-1804 90, 94
　culture 542
　current publications 539
　diplomatic archives 532
　Fifth Republic 148−149
　folklore 158
　geography 20
　historical archives 533−534
　history 45, 76, 78, 80, 518, 522, 542
　labour movements 364
　language 542
　literature 408, 426, 542
　maps and atlases 20
　Napoleon I 90
　periodical articles 541
　philosophy 181, 542
　religion 542
　Revolution, 1789 90, 94
　statistics 251
Bibliographies, National 539−540
Bibliography of French labor, with a selection of documents on the French labor movement 364
Bibliothèque Nationale 41, 535
Bichat, Xavier 398
Bidonvilles 236
Bidwell, R. 154
Bijaoui-Rosenfeld, J. 247
Billaud-Varenne, Jean Nicolas 100
Binsse, H. L. 46

Biogeography 35
Biographies, Current 528
Biography
　bibliographies 540
Births
　19th century 254
　statistics 254
Black immigrants 236
Blackmer, D. L. M. 278
Blanchot, M. 437
Bloc National 266
Bloch, M. 57−58, 126, 194, 370
Blomfield, R. 457−458
Blondel, J. 312
Blue Guide to Paris 41
Blumenthal, H. 291
Bohemian versus bourgeois: French society and the French man of letters in the nineteenth century 421
Bolshevism 119
Bonapartist party 266
Bond and equity markets 349
Bony, J. 460
Book clubs 484
Book of the Basques 156
Book of French quotations with English translations 409
Book reviews 503−504, 513, 515, 517, 524
Book trade 484−485
　bibliographies of current publications 539
Bookshops, English-language 484
Bordas encyclopédie 526
Borzoi book of French folk tales 158
Bosworth, W. 164
Bouches du Rhone 25
Boudon, Raymond 233, 262
Bouju, P. A. 36
Boulanger, Georges 119
Boulangist party 266
Bourdien, Pierre 223
Bouret, J. 447
Bourgeoisie in 18th-century France 85
Bourricaud, François 262
Boutier, Robert H. 534
Branca, P. 212, 399
Brandy 386
Bras, M. 403
Bread 389
Breads of France 389
Bree, G. 412, 432
Breed, P. F. 542
Bremond, H. 161

148

Brereton, G. 410, 477
Breton folktales 157
Bretons, The 235, 237−238, 240
 folklore 157, 159
Bretons against France: ethnic minority nationalism in twentieth-century Brittany 240
Briard, J. 42
Bridges 397
Briggs, R. 72
Brinton, C. 98, 102
Brittany 42
Brittany 42
 folklore 157, 159
 guides 39
Broadcasting reviews 515
Brogan, D. W. 47, 82, 115
Brogan, O. 53
Broome, P. 427−428
Broussard, J. 37
Brouwer, R. 275
Brown, B. E. 142
Brown, M. L. 83
Brown, R. S. 474
Brummfitt, J. H. 172
Brzezinski, Zbigniew 292
Budget, National
 19th century 310
Budgetary processes
 20th century 310
Bulletin mensuel de statistique 250
Bullough, D. A. 60
Bureaucrats 313−316
Burtenshaw, D. B. 25
Bus stop for Paris: the transformation of a French village 207
Business 352−357, 359
 19th century 358
 20th century 358
 bibliographies 540
 Vichy régime 352
Butor, Michel 435−438
Butterfield, H. 47
Byrnes, R. F. 249

C

Cali, F. 26
Camargue, The 31
Cambon, Joseph 100
Cameron, R. 346
Camp, W. D. 87
Campbell, I. 280
Campbell, P. 258, 312, 329
Campbell, Robert 183
Camus, Albert 182, 194−195, 434, 480
Canals 397
Capitalist policy
 19th century 333
 20th century 333
 history 333
Cappelle, J. 226
Cardin, Pierre 360
Carnot, Lazare 100
Carolingian Empire 59−60
Caron, F. 333
Caroutch, Yvonne 431
Carre, Jean-J. 332
Carrington, D. 30
Carroll, J. T. 18
Carter, Edward C., II 358
Cartesianism 170
Cartier, Jacques 151
Case, L. M. 532
Catalans, The 235
Cathedrals 26, 460
Catherine de Medici 67
Catholic avant-garde: French Catholicism since World War II 165
Catholic press 164, 489, 506
Catholicism
 19th century 163
 20th century 164−165, 183
 and the French State 166
Catholicism and crisis in modern France: French Catholic groups at the threshold of the Fifth Republic 164
Catholics and unbelievers in eighteenth century France 162
Caullery, M. 390
Caute, D. 276
Cavanaugh, J. F. 91
Cazeaux, I. 468
CEA 297
Celts 43−44, 52
Celts and Gallo-Romans 43
Censuses, Population 252
Centrist party 259
Ceramics 450−452
Chabrol, Claude 483
Chambre Syndicate de la Couture Parisienne 360
Champagne 387
 history 388

149

Champagne: with appendices on corks, methods of keeping and serving champagne, vintages, brands, shippers 387
Chanel, Gabrielle 360
Channel tunnel project 394
Chansons de geste 413
Chantilly 41
Chanzeaux: a village in Anjou 208
Chapman, B. 317, 321, 329
Chapman, G. 120
Charles X 110
Charlton, D. G. 180
Charvet, P. E. 3
Chateaux 26
 Loire 39
Chedid, André 431
Chemical inventions
 18th century 395
Chesters, G. 427−428
Chevallier, R. 26
Child welfare 217
The childhood of a leader 434
Children 16
Children and the law 325
Chivalrous society 65
Chivalry 61
Chivalry 61, 64−65
ˡChosisme 433
Chovin, P. 381
Chronicles, Mediaeval 413
Chronologies
 labour and politics 362
Church and State 164
 history 166
 separation, 1905-07 328
Church and state in France, 1300-1907 166
Church, W. F. 76
Cinema 10, 16, 438, 481−483
 bibliographies 540
 periodicals 508, 514
Cities 20
 plans 40
City planning 466−467
Civil Code 16, 327
Civil rights 255
Civil servants 317
 20th century 257
Civil service 312−316
Civilization
 bibliographies 542
Civilization of France 1
Clark, T. J. 445

Clark, U. 455
Class structure 19
 20th century 211, 262
Classical drama 415
Classical voices: studies of Corneille, Racine, Molière, Mme. de Lafayette 415
Classification of educational systems in OECD member countries: France, Norway, Spain 229
Claudel, Paul 425, 480
Clayton, Bernard, Jr. 389
Clergy
 18th century 84
Climate 27
 maps 35
 statistics 250, 253
Climates of Northern and Western Europe 27
Clough, S. B. 344
Clout, H. D. 25, 220
Cobb, R. 179
Cobban, Alfred 80, 91, 104, 174
Cocteau, Jean 480
Code civil 327
Code Napoléon 325
Code Napoléon and the common-law world 325
Coffey, P. 334
Cognac 386
Cohen-Portheim, P. 4
Cohen, S. S. 339
Colbert and a century of French mercantilism 342
Cold War 127
Cole, C. W. 342
Coleman, F. X. J. 175
Collapse of the Third Republic: an inquiry into the fall of France in 1940 123
Collieries 397
Collision in Brussels: the Common Market crisis of 30 June 1965 294
Colloquialisms 406
Collot d'Herbois, Jean-Marie 100
Colonial policy
 19th century 118
 20th century 118, 141
Colonialism
 20th century 153, 155
 bibliographies 152
 history 151−153, 155
Colonies 36
Coltman, D. 13, 289

150

Combat 133
Coming of the French Revolution, 1789 86
Comité National Français de Geographie 35
Commerce 353—357, 359
  19th century 345, 358
  20th century 345, 358
  bibliographies 540
  Gallo-Roman 53
  Vichy régime 352
Commercial development 355
Commissariat à l'Energie Atomique 297
Committee of Public Safety, 1793-95 100
Common law 324—326
Common Market 348
  French policy 292—294
Common Market and how it works 348
Communauté, La 296
Commune de Paris, 1871 116—117
Communes
  organization 321
Communications 18, 374—375
  statistics 250, 253
Communications industries 394
Communism and the French intellectuals, 1914-1960 276
Communism in Italy and France 278
Communist Party 189, 273—280
  newspapers 493
Competition and controls in banking: a study of the regulation of bank competition in Italy, France, and England 350
Comte, Auguste 170, 191
Concise bibliography of French literature 408
Concorde 375
Concorde conspiracy: the international race for the SST 375
Condillac, Etienne Bonnot de 170, 175—176
Condorcet, Marie Jean Antoine Caritat, marquis de 191
Confédération Générale de la Production Française 352
Confer, Vincent 532
Conflicts in French society: anticlericalism, education, and morals in the nineteenth century; essays 107
Connolly, C. 426

Conseil d'État 307—308
Conseil d'État in modern France 307
Conseil National de Patronat 352
Conservative politics in France 267
Considerable town 29
Constitution of the Fifth Republic 329
Constitutional history 303
Constitutions 324—328
  18th century 95, 97
  20th century 136, 142
  Fifth Republic 302, 304—305, 329—331, 529
  Fourth Republic 255
  history 328
Constitutions and other select documents illustrative of the history of France, 1789-1907 328
Consulat, 1799-1804
  bibliographies 90, 94
Le conte populaire Français 158
Contemporary French literature, 1945 and after 429
Contemporary French philosophy: a study in norms and values 182
Contemporary French political thought 195
Contemporary French women poets: a bilingual critical anthology 431
Contes de ma mère l'oye 159
Contract law 325
Conversation vocabularies 40
Conversational French 406
Cook and the man-eater, The 190
Cookery 382—384
  periodicals 511
Cooper, M. 472
Coping with the oil crisis: French and German experiences 380
Copyright 484
  official lists of publications issued 539
Corbett, E. M. 296
Corday d'Armont, Charlotte 101
Cordorcet, Marie Jean Antoine Caritat, marquis de 170
Corneille, Pierre 415
Corporatism 339
  history 193
Corsica 30
  folklore 159
Corsicans, The 235
Costello, J. 375
Costume 360—361
  periodicals 511, 516

Côtes-du-Nord 205
Cotton industries 353
Counterparts: the dynamics of Franco-German literary relationships, 1770-1895 416
Courrèges, Andre 360
Court life
  17th century 74—75
Courteault, H. 534
Courtly literature, Mediaeval 414
Courtly love 64
Cousin, Victor 170
Couthon, Georges 100
Couture: an illustrated history of the great Paris designers and their creations 360
Crabb, J. H. 327
Crafts
  Gallo-Roman 52
Credit institutions 349, 351
Crisis and compromise: politics in the Fourth Republic 263
Croissants 389
Cronin, Vincent 197
Cros, Charles 427
Crosbie, S. K. 295
Crosland, J. 413
Crosland, M. 391—392
Crosten, W. L. 470
Crousaz, Jean Pierre de 175
Crozier, B. 147
Crozier, M. 188, 210
Cuisenier, J. 160
Culinary terms 383—384
Cultural relations
  with EEC members 292
  with Germany 301
  with the USA 290—291
Culture 1, 4—6, 10—11, 13—16, 19, 36—37, 50, 81, 83
  16th century 67—71
  17th century 73—75
  18th century 84
  19th century 114
  20th century 114, 137, 144, 188, 228
  bibliographies 542
  Carolingian 60
  history 45, 48, 169
  periodicals 525
Culture of France in our time 6
Current events
  periodicals 504, 507, 512—513
Curtius, E. R. 1
Customs and Economic Union of Central Africa 296

D

Dada, surrealism, and their heritage 449
Dadaism 449, 479
Daily life in the world of Charlemagne 59
Dale, L. A. 364
Dances of England and France from 1450-1600: with their music and authentic manner of performance 475
Dances, Renaissance 475
Daniels, G. 44
Dank, M. 131
Darby, H. C. 47
Daumier, Honoré 445
Dauphiné
  folklore 159
Daval, R. 169
David, R. 324
Davies, J. 349
De Gaulle 147
De Gaulle and the Anglo-Saxons 288
De Gaulle and the world: the foreign policy of the Fifth French Republic 285
De Gaulle, Charles 142—147, 150, 271, 284—288, 294
De Gaulle republic: quest for unity 142
Death
  16th century attitudes 71
Debussy, Claude 471, 473
Decade of revolution, 1789-1799 98
Decline of French patriotism, 1870-1940 119
Decline or renewal? France since the 1930s 150
Decorating, Interior
  periodicals 511
Defence industries 394
Defence policies 297—299
Delacroix, Eugène 445
Delamotte, Y. 369
Delarue, Paul 158—159
Democracy in France since 1870 196
Democratic theory
  19th century 196
  20th century 196—197
Demography 36
Demuth, N. 469
Denieul-Cormier, A. 68
Denomme, R. T. 423—424
Departmental archives 534

Deputies of the National
  Assembly 309
Derivry, Daniel 315
Deroulède, Paul 119
Derrida, Jacques 185
Descartes, René 170
Desnos, Robert 427
*Development of French Romanticism:
  the impact of the industrial
  revolution on literature* 420
*Development of modern France,
  1870-1939* 115
Dictionaries 404—405
  bibliographies 540
  scientific and technical
    abbreviations 407
Dictionaries, Technical 407
Didactic literature, Mediaeval 413
Diderot, Denis 175
d'Indy, Vincent 471
Dior, Christian 360
Diplomatic and consular service 283
Diplomatic archives
  bibliographies 532
Diplomatic history 45
*Direction des Bibliothèques et de la
  Lecture Publique* 537
Directories 528—529
Discovering the Camargue 31
Docks 397
Documentation centres
  directories 535
Dogan, M. 315
Dollfuss, J. 23
Dolmetsch, M. 475
Domenach, Jean-Marie 165, 506
Dorson, Richard M. 159
*Dossiers et Documents du Monde,
  Les* 541
Douglass, William A. 237
Doukas, K. A. 376
Doumec, R. M. 379
Drama
  16th century 477
  17th century 477—478
  20th century 429, 479—480
  bibliographies 540
  classical 415
  history 429, 477—480
  periodicals 514
Drama reviews 513
Dress 360—361
  periodicals 511, 516
Dreyfus, Alfred 119—120, 249
Dreyfus case: a reassessment 120

Drink 385—388
Drinking, Excessive 216
Drinking in French culture 216
Drinking patterns 216
Du Bos, Charles 430
Dualism
  20th century 182
Dubois, M. M. 404
Dubois, P. 332
Dubuis, J. 246
Duby, G. 48, 65
Dumery, Henry 183
Dunbar, J. 383
Dunning, D. C. 61
Duras, Marguerite 437
Duroselle, Jean-B. 15, 261, 289
Duverger, M. 255

E

Earle, E. M. 137
Early medieval history 56
Early modern France, 1560-1715 72
Echos, Les 496
Ecological movements 377
Ecology 377—379, 381
Economic anthropology 184
Economic development 2, 10, 15, 24
  17th century 342
  19th century 333, 344—345, 372
  20th century 136—137, 332—333,
    341, 344—345, 372
  Fifth Republic 334, 336—339
  Fourth Republic 335—339
  history 332—339, 342, 344—346
  population movements 340
  statistics 341
Economic geography 35—36
*Economic growth in France and
  Britain, 1851-1950* 345
Economic history 81, 83
*Economic history of modern
  France* 333
Economic institutions 334
*Economic planning: the French
  experience* 338
Economic planning in France 337
Economic resources
  statistics 250
Economic theory
  corporatism 193
Economics 19, 332—348
  16th century 66
  17th century 72

153

Economics *contd.*
  18th century 176
  historiography 346
  history 169
  Marxist influence 189
EDC
  French policy 299
Education 6, 18, 36, 50, 312
  18th century 176
  19th century 107, 113, 223—224
  20th century 222—229
  Carolingian 60
  Catholic 164—165
  history 221
  periodicals 515
  statistics 253
Education and change in a village community: Mazières-en-Gatine, 1848-1914 113
Education and the French Revolution 221
Education and society in modern France 225
Education, culture and politics in modern France 228
Education for women
  17th century 75
Education in France 222
Educational policy and planning: France 227
Educational reform 223, 225—228, 231, 233—234
Egalitarianism
  18th century 85
Egret, J. 87
Ehrmann, H. W. 352, 363
Einaudi, L. 2
Elbow, M. H. 193
Elections
  19th century 118, 258
  20th century 118, 258
  Fifth Republic 259, 304
  Fourth Republic 264
Electoral systems
  19th century 258
  20th century 258
  Fifth Republic 304
Electronics industry 355—357
Elgey, G. 129
Elites in French society: the politics of survival 211
Ellis, Major L. F. 125
Elson, Brigid 165

Eluard, Paul 427
Emergence of science in Western Europe 392
Emigration
  to the USA 290
Employers' associations 352
Employment 347
Encyclopaedias 526—527
  bibliographies 540
Energy
  1985 plan 379
  EEC policies 378
  policy 380
Energy and the European communities 378
Engler, W. 417
Englishmen, Frenchmen, Spaniards 11
Enlightenment 171
Enlightenment, The 78, 162, 171—177, 395
Enterprise and entrepreneurs in nineteenth- and twentieth-century France 358
Entertainment 5, 9, 18
Environment 22, 25, 377—381
Era of the French Revolution, 1789-1799: ten years that shook the world 97
Escoffier, A. 384
Escoffier cook book: a guide to the fine art of cookery 384
Essays in French economic history 346
État des inventaires des archives nationales, départementales, communales et hospitalières, au 1er janvier 1937 534
Ethics
  18th century 177
Ethnic groups 235—246
Eurocommunism 279
Europe against De Gaulle 143
Europe from below: an assessment of Franco-German popular contacts 301
European administrative élite 313
European advanced technology: a programme for integration 394
European Defence Community
  French policy 299
European Economic Community 143, 348
  French policy 292—294

European historical statistics, 1750-1970 253
European money puzzle 349
European perspectives in teacher education 231
Evans, E. M. 93
Evans, J. 440, 462
Examination systems 229, 232
Existential Marxism in postwar France: from Sartre to Althusser 200
Existentialism 182−183, 200, 430

F

Factories 397
Fall of Paris, the siege and the Commune, 1870-71 117
Family life 16
Farber, M. 183
Farming 370−373
Farquharson, J. E. 301
Fascism 119, 266, 270
Fashion 360−361
  designers 360−361
  periodicals 511, 516
Fath, Jacques 360
Fauré, Gabriel 471, 473
Faure, Olivier 399
Favier, Jean 518
Faye, Jean Pierre 437
February Revolution 111−112
Febvre, Lucien 70, 194, 370
Federalism
  20th century 143
Female population of France in the nineteenth century: a reconstruction of 82 departments 254
Ferguson, J. 537
Ferlin, M. 405
Fertility
  19th century 254
  statistics 254
Feudal society 57
Feudalism 57−58
  18th century 178
Fiction 438
  19th century 419
  20th century 429
  bibliographies 540
  history 417−419, 422, 429, 432−437

Fielding, A. 340
Fife, Austin 158
Fifth French Republic 302
Fifth Republic
  bibliographies 148−149
  constitution 142
  history 142−146
Figaro Littéraire, Le 491
Film reviews 513, 515
Films 10, 16, 481−483
  bibliographies 540
  periodicals 508, 514
Finance 341, 349−351
  19th century 310, 345
  20th century 310, 332, 345
  history 332
  statistics 250, 253
Financial administration 312
Finistère 205
Fisher, M. F. K. 29
Fisher, Sydney Nettleton 292
Fisheries
  statistics 250
Flaubert, Gustave 418, 421−422
Flemish, The 235
Fleur de lys: the kings and queens of France 51
Fleury, André Hercule, cardinal de 84
Floralies, Les 215
Fodor's France 40
Folk art 160
Folk dances
  Basque 156
Folk songs
  Basque 156
Folklore
  Basque 156
  bibliographies 158
  Breton 157, 159
  French 158−159
Folktales of France 159
Fontainebleau 41
Fontenelle, Bernard le Bovier de 170
Food 382−384, 389
Food of France 382
Foot, M. R. D. 135
Forbes, P. 405
Force de frappe policy 297−298
Foreign affairs 282−289, 292−296, 298−301
  Russia 83
Foreign Legion, The 218−219
Foreign Office
  archival collections 532

155

Foreign policy
  19th century 118
  20th century 15, 118, 136—137, 145, 150, 282—288, 300
  Fifth Republic 302, 304
  with the EEC 292
  with Germany 301
  with Great Britain 288
  with Israel 295
  with the Middle East 295
  with the USA 288—289
Foreign policy and interdependence in Gaullist France 287
Foreign policy of France from 1914 to 1945 282
Forestry
  statistics 250
Forez
  folklore 159
Forster, Robert 358
Fortier, David H. 237
Founding of the French Socialist Party, 1893-1905 272
Foundries 397
Fourest, Henri-P. 452
Fourier, Charles 191
Fourth Republic 7
  history 127, 136—137
Fowlie, W. 411
Français dans le Monde, Le 541
France 3, 22, 144, 465
France, 1848-1945 114
France, 1870-1914: politics and society 118
France, 1940-1955 127
France: a geographical study 21
France, a geographical survey 20
France: a history of national economics, 1789-1939 344
France: a modern history 49
France: a short history 49
France: a study in nationality 8
France against herself: a perceptive study of France's past, her politics, and her unending crises 12
France and the Africans, 1944-1960: a political history 153
France and Britain in Africa: imperial rivalry and colonial rule 152
France and the European Community 292
France and the United States: from the beginnings to the present day 289

France before the Romans 44
France between the republics 128
France defeats EDC 299
La France des minorités 235
La France étrangère 236
France from the air 26
France: government and society; an historical survey 303
France in the 16th century: a medieval society transformed 67
France in the age of Louis XIII and Richelieu 77
France in the age of the scientific state 393
France in modern times: 1760 to the present 78
France in the twentieth century 19
France: an interpretive history 45
France: its geography and growth 23
France since 1789 81
France since the Revolution 79
France-Soir 498
France, steadfast and changing 2
Franche-Comté
  folklore 159
Francis I 67
Franco-Belgian border 25
The Franco-Belgium border region 25
Franco-German War, 1870-71 117
Franco-Moroccan conflict, 1941-1956 154
Frankish Gaul 55
Franks, The 54—55
Fraser, W. R. 225
Frears, J. 17
Frears, J. R. 259
Frédégaire 55
Freedman, C. E. 307
Fremantle, A. 68
Fremantle, C. 68
Frenay, H. 133
French administrative law and the common-law world 326
French against the French: collaboration and resistance 131
French army in politics, 1945-1962 265
French banking structure and credit policy 351
French budgetary process 310
French cathedrals 460
French ceramics 452
French chivalry: chivalric ideas and practices in mediaeval France 64
French cinema since 1946 481

French Civil Code: as amended to
 July 1, 1976 327
French civil service 316
French colonialism in tropical Africa,
 1900-1945 155
French communism, 1920-1972 274
French communism in the making,
 1914-1924 275
French Communist Party in transition:
 PCF-CPSU relations and the
 challenge to Soviet authority 279
French communists: profile of a
 people 277
French corporative theory, 1789-1948:
 a chapter in the history of
 ideas 193
French decorative art, 1638-1793 450
French democracy 197
French democratic Left, 1963-1969:
 toward a modern party
 system 281
French deputy: incentives and behavior
 in the National Assembly 309
French economic growth 332
French economy and the state 335
French education since Napoleon 223
French electoral systems and elections
 since 1789 258
French-English science and technology
 dictionary 407
French Enlightenment 172
French fiction today: a new
 direction 437
French Fifth Republic: continuity and
 change, 1966-1970; an annotated
 bibliography 149
French Fifth Republic: establishment
 and consolidation, 1958-1965; an
 annotated bibliography of the
 holdings at the Hoover
 Institution 148
French film 482
French folk art 160
French Foreign Legion 218−219
French foreign policy since the Second
 World War 283
French foreign policy under De
 Gaulle 284
French formal garden, The 454
French garden, 1500-1800 454
French grand opera: an art and a
 business 470
French historical method: the Annales
 paradigm 187
French: how they live and work 18

French humanism, 1470-1600 69
French international policy under De
 Gaulle and Pompidou: the politics
 of grandeur 286
French inventions of the
 eighteenth-century 395
French labor from Popular Front to
 Liberation 363
French labor movement 362
French language 401−407
 history 400
French language teaching
 periodicals 509, 521, 523
French law: its structure, sources and
 methodology 324
French liberal thought in the
 eighteenth century: a study of
 political ideas from Bayle to
 Condorcet 192
French literature 409−438
 bibliographies 408
French literature: its history and
 meaning 411
French medicine 398
French mercantilism, 1683-1700 342
French mercantilist doctrines before
 Colbert 342
French music: from the death of
 Berlioz to the death of Fauré 472
French music in the fifteenth and
 sixteenth centuries 468
French nation from Napoleon to
 Pétain, 1814-1940 82
French new novel: Claude Simon,
 Michel Butor, Alain
 Robbe-Grillet 435
French new towns 466
French novel: from Eighteen Hundred
 to the present 417
French novel from Gide to Camus 432
French novelists speak out 438
French nuclear diplomacy 298
French opera: its development to the
 Revolution 469
French painting 441
French parliament 305
French Parnassian poets 424
French political system 255
French politics: the first years of the
 Fourth Republic 136
French polity 260
French, portrait of a people 5
French prerevolution, 1787-1788 87
French presence in Black Africa 296

French prophets of yesterday: a study of religious thought under the Second Empire 163
French railroads and the state 376
French reference grammar for schools and colleges 402
French resistance, 1940 to 1944 132
French Revolution 88, 92—93, 95
French Revolution: a concise history 96
French Revolution and Napoleon collection at Florida State University: a bibliographical guide 90
French Revolution and Napoleon; with a new annotated bibliography 94
French Revolution: conflicting interpretations 89
French Revolution of 1830 110
French rural history: an essay on its basic characteristics 370
French science and its principal discoveries since the seventeenth century 390
French Second Republic: a social history 111
French society and culture since the old régime 83
French stake in Algeria, 1945-1962 141
French student uprising, November 1967-June 1968: an analytical record 234
French tapestry 453
French thought in the eighteenth century 177
French tradition in education: Ramus to Mme. Necker de Saussure 221
French tragic drama in the sixteenth and seventeenth centuries 477
French Union 2
French utopias: an anthology of ideal societies 191
Freud, Sigmund 185—186
Friguglietti, J. 93
From Sartre to the new novel 434
Furet, F. 88
Furniture 450
Furst, L. R. 416

G

Gagnon, Paul 49, 81
Gallo-Roman civilization 43, 52—53

Gallup, R. 156
Galton, A. 166
Gambetta, Léon 119
Gardens
  history 454, 463
Gardinier, David 152
Gardner, R. K. 538
Gastronomy 382—383
Gates of horn: a study of five French realists 422
Gauguin, Paul 444
Gaullism: the rise and fall of a political movement 271
Gaullist party 259, 271, 305
Gauls 44
Gautier, L. 61
Gautier, Théophile 424
Gaxotte, Pierre 98
General says no 293
Genet, Jean 480
Geneva school 430
Gennep, Arnold van 159
Geography 18—19, 21—27, 29—41
  bibliographies 20, 540
  social 28
  statistics 250
Geometric spirit: the Abbé de Condillac and the French Enlightenment 176
Geomorphology 35
George, A. J. 420
George, P. 21
Germany
  impact of French culture 301
Gershoy, L. 94, 97
Geyl, P. 105
Gide, André 276
Giele, J. Z. 213
Gifford, P. 152
Gilpin, R. 393
Le gimmick: français parlé 406
Giot, P. R. 42
Giraudoux, Jean 480
Girondins 104
Girondist movement 104
Giscard d'Estaing, Valéry 197, 300
Giscardien party 259
Glossary of French literary expression 401
Glucksmann, André 190
Godard, Jean-Luc 483
Gode, A. 417
Goguel, F. 15
Gombin, R. 201
Goncourt, Edmond 418

Goncourt, Jules 418
Goreux, L. M. 372
Gothic architecture 459
Gothic cathedrals of France 461
Gottheimer, T. 155
Goubert, Jean-Pierre 399
Goubet, S. 461
Gourevitch, Peter 262
Gourmont, Remy de 430
Government 18—19
 15th century 62
 17th century 76
 19th century 108
 20th century 2
 bibliographies 540
 directories 529
 Fifth Republic 306
 Fourth Republic 318
 history 79
 Third Republic 320
Government and commerce 355
Government and industry 355, 357, 369
Government and politics of France 302, 304
Government and society 303
 Fifth Republic 306
 Fourth Republic 319
Government and technocracy 311
Government in France: an introduction to the executive power 306
Government institutions
 Fifth Republic 260, 302, 304
 Fourth Republic 255
Government of the French [Third] Republic 320
Grammar 402, 404
Gramont, Sanche de 5
Grana, C. 421
Grand opera 470
La grande encyclopédie 526
Granick, D. 354
Granite island: a portrait of Corsica 30
Grant, P. 217
Grappe, Denise 431
Great wave: the influence of Japanese woodcuts on French prints 444
Greaves, R. 26
Greene, T. H. 273
Greenlaw, R. W. 103
Gregoire, R. 316
Gregory of Tours 54—55
Grodecki, L. 459
Grosser, A. 284

Growth of European mixed economies, 1945-1970: a concise study of the economic evolution of six countries 336
Guerard, A. L. 49, 163
Guest, I. 476
Guicharnaud, J. 480
Guide culinaire 384
Guide to the diplomatic archives of Western Europe 532
Guide to the industrial archaeology of Europe 397
Guides, Tourist 38—41
Guiton, M. 432
Gundetscheimer, W. L. 69
Gunn, J. A. 181
Guterman, N. 409
Gutkind, E. 467

H

Hackett, Anne-M. 337
Hackett, J. 337
Hahn, R. 392
Hallmark, R. E. 71
Halls, W. D. 226, 228
Halperin, E. 277
Hamilton, R. F. 264
Hampden Jackson, J. 47
Hampson, N. 96, 171
Handbook on France 47
Handicapped, The 217
Hardman, S. 88
Hare, H. 129
Harrap's shorter French and English dictionary 405
Harris, A. 4
Hartley, A. 271
Harvey, D. J. 79
Hatfield, J. P. 332
Hatt, Jean-J. 43
Haute couture 360
Hazelhurst, F. Hamilton 454
Heath, Stephen 435
Heinz, G. 148—149
Henri IV 67
Henry, Jean 183
Héraut de Séchelles, Marie Jean 100
Heredia, José Marie de 424
Hérier, Thomas 399
Hermey, C. 431
Higher education 229—230, 232
Highways, International 374
Higonnet, P. L. R. 206

159

Hill, Edward Burlingame 471
Hincmar, Archbishop 55
Hirsch Plan, 1951-57 336
Histoire de l'enseignement en France, 1800-1967 224
Histoire des idées en France 169
Historia Francorum 54
Historical archives
  bibliographies 533—534
Historical geography 36—37
Historiography
  Annales school 187, 194
  Marxist influence 189
History
  17th century 72—77
  18th century 84—106, 176
  19th century 82, 107—120, 180
  20th century 114—115, 118—119, 121—146, 148—155
  bibliographies 45, 76, 78, 80, 518, 522, 540, 542
  Fourth Republic 7
  from 1715 78—81, 83
  general 12, 46—51
  Middle Ages 54—65
  periodicals 510, 518, 522
  Renaissance 66—68, 70—71
  Roman-Gaul 52—53
History makers: the press of Europe from its beginnings through 1965 486
History of architecture in France 456
History of champagne: with notes on the other sparkling wines 388
History of France 46
History of the Franks 54
History of French architecture 457
History of French civilization 48
History of the French language 400
History of Impressionism 446
History of modern France 80
History of modern philosophy in France 170
History of Protestantism 167
Hochman, Stanley 407
Hoffmann, S. 15, 146, 150, 330
Hofstadter, D. 133
Hogarth, J. 43
Holt, S. C. 301
Hoover Institution, Library
  Fifth Republic holdings 148—149
Hopkins, G. 46, 126
Horne, A. 117, 122, 139
Horward, D. D. 90
Hotels 38

Housing 18
Houston, J. 22
How to find out about France: a guide to sources of information 540
Hudson, K. 397
Hughes, H. S. 194
Hughes, T. 375
Hugo, Victor 418, 423, 427
Huguenot Wars 66
Human geography 35
Human rights 255
  18th century 192
  mediaeval 58
Humanism
  16th century 69
  19th century 163
  history 161, 163
Humanité-Dimanche 493
Hunt, A. J. 20
Hunter, M. 383
Hurlimann, M. 460
Hydrography 35
Hyland, J. 159

I

Idealism 191
Ideologists, The 170
Idiom 406
Île de la Camargue 31
Illustrations
  aerial photographs 26
  history 37
  Revolution 1789 96
Immigrants 236, 243—247
Impact of absolutism in France: national experience under Richelieu, Mazarin, and Louis XIV 76
Imperial role
  20th century 153, 155
  history 151—153, 155
Impressionism
  history 446
In first gear: the French automobile industry to 1914 359
In the labyrinth 434
In search of France 15
In search of humanity: the role of the Enlightenment in modern history 174
Incomes
  statistics 250

Independence movements
　ethnic groups 235
Individualism 8
Indochina, French
　20th century 127
Industrial development 10, 355
Industrial equipment industries 353
*Industrial policies in Western
　Europe* 357
Industrial reform
　20th century 369
Industry 18, 20, 352, 355—359
　17th century 73
　18th century 84
　19th century 345
　20th century 345, 353
　bibliographies 540
　Gallo-Roman 53
　management 354
　statistics 250, 253
Inebriates 216
Inflation 336, 347
*Inflation and unemployment in France:
　a quantitative analysis* 347
INSEE 250
Institut Géographique National
　maps 32—33
Institut National de la Statistique et
　des Études Économiques 251
*Institutions sociales de la France,
　Les* 217
Intellectuals
　20th century 188, 276
　political attitudes 276
Interior decoration 450
Interior, Ministry of the
　organization 321
*International economy and monetary
　movements in France,
　1493-1725* 343
International highways 374
International relations 282—289,
　292—296, 298—301
*Introduction to eighteenth-century
　France* 84
*Introduction to French local
　government* 321
Introduction to the French theatre 478
*Introduction to modern France,
　1500-1640; an essay in historical
　psychology* 71
*Introduction to seventeenth-century
　France* 73
Inventions 390
　18th century 395

Investment banking 351
Ionesco, Eugène 480
Irwin, J. 2
Ives, Colta Feller 444

J

Jacobin movement 97, 102
*Jacobins: an essay in the new
　history* 102
Jacquelin, L. 385
Japanese woodcuts
　influence on French art 444
Jellinek, F. 116
Jeune Afrique 541
Jews 247—248
Johnson, D. 144
Jolas, M. 234
Jones, Howard Mumford 290
Jouvenel, Bertrand de 195
Joyce, M. H. 167
July Revolution 110
Jura region
　witchcraft 168
Justice 312
Juvenile delinquency 217

K

Kafker, F. A. 89
Kaplan, R. 190
Kelly, D. 414
Kerr, A. J. C. 348
Kesselman, M. 322
Kindergarten 222
Kindleberger, C. P. 15, 345
Kindred, M. 324
Knapp, Bettina Liebowitz 438
Knapton, E. J. 45
Knight, F. 132
Knight, I. F. 176
Knighthood 61, 64—65
Knowledge
　20th century 183
Knox, P. L. 28
Kochan, L. 461
Kochan, M. 461
Kohl, W. L. 298
Kolodziej, E. A. 286
Kriegel, A. 277
Krippner, M. 31
Krumbhaar, E. B. 398
Kulski, W. W. 285

L

Labor movement in post-war France, The 363
Labour
  statistics 253
Labour and politics
  chronologies 362
Labour movements
  19th century 199, 362, 365, 368
  20th century 362−363, 368
  bibliographies 364
Labour problems 347
Lacan, Jacques 185
L'Actualité 541
Laennec, René 398
Lafayette, Marie-Madeleine, comtesse de 415
Laffin, J. 219
Laforgue, Jules 427
Laignel-Lavastine, M. 398
Lamartine, Alphonse de 423
Lambert, E. 361
Landau, D. 210
Landscape
  aerial photographs 26
Laney, A. 487
Langlois, C. V. 533
Language 5, 18
  17th century 73
  bibliographies 540, 542
Language of French symbolism 425
Languedociens, The 235
Larmour, P. 145
Laroque, P. 217
Larousse modern French-English, English-French dictionary 404
Later medieval France: the polity 62
Lauter, Robert S. 233
Laux, J. M. 89, 266, 359
Lavers, A. 9
Law 6, 50, 324−327, 329−331
  history 328
  interpretation 307−308
Law courts 326
Law, J. 51
Lawler, J. 425
Lawyers 324
Layton, C. 394
Layton, T. A. 385
Leclaire, Serge 185
Leconte de Lisle, Charles Marie 424
Ledesert, D. M. 405
Ledesert, R. P. 405
Lefebvre, G. 86, 93

Lefebvre, Henri 183
Left-wing parties 259, 272−275, 277−280
  Fifth Republic 261−262, 281
Legal training 324
Légion étrangère 218−219
Legislation 307−308
Legitimist party 266
Leites, N. C. 13, 319
Lejard, A. 453
Lemay, Edna Hindle 399
Leonard, E. G. 167
Lerner, D. 299
Lerner, J. 203
Les archives de l'histoire de France: manuels de bibliographie historique 533
Lévi-Strauss, Claude 184, 194
Levin, H. 422
Levin, L. M. 177
Levitte, G. 247
Levran, J. 61
Lévy, Bernard-Henri 190
Lévy-Bruhl, L. 170
Lewis, P. 62
Lewis, W. H. 75
Lex Salica 55
L'Express 541
L'Helgouach, J. 42
Liberalism
  18th century 192
  20th century 197
Libraries 41
  directories 535−537
  Hoover Institution 148−149
  Paris 536, 538
  reorganization 538
  Stozier Library 90
  terminology 536
Libraries in France 537
Libraries in Paris: a student's guide 536
Lichine, A. 386
Lichtheim, G. 199
Lidderdale, D. W. S. 318
Lieberman, S. 336
Life and customs 18, 50
  16th century 70
  Carolingian 59
  Gallo-Roman 53
  mediaeval 57
Life assurance 349
Life in Renaissance France 70
Lighting
  18th century 395

Ligue des Patriotes 119
Limits of integration: ethnicity and nationalism in modern Europe 237
Limousin
 folklore 159
Lindet, Robert 100
Lindsay, N. 217
Linguistics
 18th century 176
 Marxist influence 189
Literary criticism 429—430
 Marxist influence 189
Literary history
 bibliographies 540
Literary history of religious thought in France 161
Literary quotations 409
Literary terminology 401
Literature 6, 50, 409, 412, 417—418, 422—425, 427—428, 430—438
 12th century 413—414
 13th century 413—414
 16th century 67
 17th century 73, 75, 415
 18th century 84
 19th century 416, 419—421
 20th century 429
 bibliographies 408, 426, 540, 542
 German 19th century influences 416
 history 410—411, 413—416, 419—421, 429
 periodicals 514, 517, 519, 524
Literature and society 410, 419—421, 445
Liturgy, Mediaeval 469
Living standards 28, 334
Livres de l'Année-Biblio, Les 539
Livres du Mois 539
Lloyd, A. 356
Local government 312, 321—323
 20th century 256
 Fifth Republic 262
 finance 321
Lockie, D. McN. 77
Loire
 guides 39
Lolli, G. 216
Lomax, D. E. 231
Long-haired kings and other studies in Frankish history 55
Loomis, S. 101
Lord, G. 310
Lorrains, The 235
Lorwin, V. 362

Lottman, H. R. 484—485
Lough, J. 73, 84
Louis-Philippe 111
Louis, W. R. 152
Louis XIII 77
Louis XIV 74—76
Louis XV 84
Louis XVI 84
Louvre 41
The Lower Rhone and Marseille 25
Lucas, N. J. D. 378
Luethy, H. 12
Lully, Jean-Baptiste 469
Lutheranism 167
Lyman, T. W. 160
Lynam, R. 360

M

McBurney, C. 44
McCloy, S. T. 395
MacDougall, Elizabeth B. 454
Machin, Howard 262
MacKendrick, P. 52
Mackrell, J. Q. C. 178
McLellan, D. S. 244
McManners, J. 303
McNamara, J. A. 59
MacRae, Duncan 319
Macridis, R. C. 142
Madariaga, Salvador de 11
Magazines
 Catholic 506
 cinema 508
 for women 505, 511
 monthly 503—504, 506, 511, 514
 on culture 525
 on French language teaching 509, 521, 523
 on history 510, 518, 522
 on literature 519, 524
 on politics 520
 on social sciences 520
 on social services 519
 television 508
 twice-monthly 517
 weekly 502, 505, 507, 512—513, 515
Mahaffey, D. 408
Maine de Biran, François Pierre Gontier 170
Mâle, E. 439
Male, G. A. 222
Malebranche, Nicolas de 170
Malinvaud, E. 332

Mallarmé, Stéphane 425, 427
Mallet-Joris, Françoise 438
Malmaison 41
Malraux, André 194, 276
Management 354
Managerial comparisons of four developed countries: France, Britain, United States, Russia 354
Mandarins of Western Europe: the political roles of top civil servants 315
Mandrou, R. 48, 71
Mannequins 360
Manpower 24
Mansion, J. E. 402, 405
Manuel, F. E. 191
Manuel, F. P. 191
Manufactures 352—353
Manyon, L. A. 57
Maps and atlases 32—37
bibliographies 20
Marcel, Gabriel 194
Marczewski, J. 347
Marie Antoinette 84
Marie-France 505
Maritain, Jacques 194
Mark, I. 459
Markham, F. M. H. 106
Marseilles 25, 29
Martin du Gard, Roger 194
Martin, G. D. 429
Martin, K. 192
Marxism 189—190, 197, 199—200
Marxism in modern France 199
Marxism-Leninism 201
Mason, Edward 116
Massif Central 25
folklore 159
Massignon, G. 159
Master thinkers, The 190
Mathiez, Albert 92, 98
Matthews, J. H. 479
Mauriac, Claude 436—437
Maurois, A. 46
Maurras, Charles 270
Mayo, P. E. 238
Mayors 322—323
Mazarin, Jules, cardinal 76
Mazières-en-Gatine 113
Mead, M. 16
Medhurst, K. 239
Medicine
17th century 75
18th century 395, 399

19th century 399
history 398—399
Medicine show: patients, physicians and the perplexities of the health revolution in modern society 399
Medieval French literature 413
Medieval imagination 414
Megalithic monuments 42
Mehlman, J. 185
Mélanges historiques 58
Melodrama
19th century 419
Mendels, F. F. 346
Mendershausen, H. 380
Mendras, H. 203
Menhirs 42
Mercantilism
17th century 342
Mercier, V. 436
Mérimée, Prosper 418
Merleau-Ponty, Maurice 194, 430
Merovingians, The 54—55
Merz, G. 530
Messiaen, Olivier 473
Metalwork 450
Metaphysics
history 169
Metraux, R. 16
Meuss, R. E. K. 157
Meyerbeer, Giacomo 470
Michaux, Henri 427
Michel, A. 245
Michelet, Guy 262
Michelin Green Guide series 39
Michelin Red Guide: France 38
Middle Ages 57—58, 61, 64—65
Middle classes 15
18th century 85, 103
20th century 210, 262
Migration 220
Migration in post-war Europe: geographical essays 220
Militant hackwriter; French popular literature 1800-1848: its influence, artistic and political 419
Military affairs
20th century 137
Military inventions
18th century 395
Military politics
20th century 265
Millard, G. 461
Millet, Jean-François 445
Ministère des Affaires Etrangères
archival collections 532

Minor, L. W. 419
Mitchell, B. R. 253
Mitford, N. 74
Modern capitalist planning: the French model 339
Modern Europe: an anthropological perspective 202
Modern France: a companion to French studies 50
Modern France: a social and economic geography 24
Modern France: problems of the Third and Fourth Republics 137
Modern French criticism from Proust and Valéry to structuralism 430
Modern French music 471
Modern French music: from Fauré to Boulez 473
Modern French painters 442
Modern French philosophy: a study of the development since Comte 181
Modern French theatre from Giraudoux to Genet 480
Modern movement: one hundred key books from England, France, and America, 1880-1950 426
Modernity and its discontents 421
Modernization of North African families in the Paris area 245
Molière, Jean-Baptiste Poquelin 415, 478
Molinery, R. 398
Monaco, J. 483
Monarchist movements 119
Monarchy 51
 15th century 62
 16th century 67
 absolutism 72−73, 76
Monasteries 26
 architecture 462
Monastic architecture in France from the Renaissance to the Revolution 462
Monde de l'Education, Le 541
Monde Hebdomadaire, Le 541
Monetary policy
 16th century 343
 17th century 343
Money 349−350
Monnet, Jean 143
Monnet Plan, 1947-52 336
Monter, E. W. 168
Montesquieu, Charles, baron 170
Montgomery, K. L. 161
Montherlant, Henri de 480

Montralon, Robert de 165
Moody, J. N. 223, 358
Morals
 19th century 107
Morat, Jean-Paul 101
Morgan, Ted 5
Morin, E. 209
Mornet, D. 177
Morocco
 20th century 154
 history 154
 tribal administration 154
Morocco under colonial rule: French administration of tribal areas, 1912-1956 154
Morse, E. L. 287
Mortimer, E. 153
Mosbacher, E. 12
Moss, B. H. 365
Mounier, B. 246
Mounier, Emmanuel 195, 506
Mouvements Unis de la Résistance 134
Museums 41
 directories 530−531
 science and technology 397
Music 6, 50, 469−470, 475−476
 15th century 468
 16th century 468
 19th century 471−472
 20th century 471−474
 bibliographies 540
 history 468, 471−474
 periodicals 514
 recordings 474
 Renaissance 468
Music and society 468
 19th century 476
Music reviews 513
Musset, Alfred de 423
Myers, R. 473
Mysticism
 history 161
Mythologies 9

N

Napoleon and the awakening of Europe 106
Napoleon: for and against 105
Napoleon I 94, 105−106
 bibliographies 90

National Archives 533—534
National Assembly
  Deputies 309
National Atlas 35
National bibliographies 539—540
National character 1, 3—5, 8—9,
  11—15, 17, 144
National Plan
  Fifth Republic 310
Nationalism
  18th century 95, 177
  19th century 196
  20th century 121, 143, 196
*Nationalist revival in France,
  1905-1914* 121
NATO
  French policy 286
Natural resources
  statistics 250
Navy 50
Nere, J. 282
Nerval, Gérard de 427
New France 10, 14
New French architecture 464
*New guide to the diplomatic archives
  of Western Europe* 532
*New Jacobins: the French Communist
  Party and the Popular Front,
  1934-1938* 275
New Larousse gastronomique 383
New Left movement 200—201
*New novel from Queneau to
  Pinget* 436
*The new pilgrim: youth protest in
  transition* 233
*New wave: Truffaut, Godard, Chabrol,
  Rohmer, Rivette* 483
Newhouse, J. 288, 294
Newman, L. M. 536
Newspapers
  19th century 487
  20th century 487
  bibliographies 540
  Catholic press 489
  Communist Party 493
  English-language 487, 494
  evening 492
  financial 496
  history 486—487
  labour movements 364
  Paris 488—489, 491—496, 498
  provincial 490, 497, 499—501
  Sunday 493
  weekly 491

Night will end 133
*Nineteenth-century French Romantic
  poets* 423
Noblemen 65
  17th century 73
  18th century 84
  and commerce 178
  mediaeval 64
Noland, A. 272
Nolte, E. 270
Norman Empire 63
Normandy 63
  guides 39
Normans, The 63
North America
  French possessions history 151
North, B. 255
North, R. 255
Nouveau roman, The 435
Nouvel Observateur, Le 541
Novels 438
  19th century 419
  20th century 429
  bibliographies 540
  history 417—419, 422, 429, 432—437
NRF 514
Nuclear deterrant policy 297—298
Nuclear programme 394
Nurse, P. H. 415
Nursery schools 222

O

O'Ballance, E. 138
*Obstructed path: French social thought
  in the years of desperation,
  1930-1960* 194
Occult
  19th century 180
Office workers 210
Oil supplies
  policy 380
*Old age in European society: the case
  of France* 214
*Old people, new lives: community
  creation in a retirement
  residence* 215
Ollier, Francois 437
Olson, K. E. 486
On the game of politics in France 319
Opera
  19th century 470
  20th century 473
  history 469—470, 473

Oppeneau, Jean-C. 381
Organisation Commune Africaine et Malgache 296
Organized business in France 352
Origins of the French labor movement: the socialism of skilled workers, 1830-1906 365
Origins of modern leftism 201
Orleanist party 266
Ouston, P. 19
Overseas aid 283

P

Paganism
 19th century 180
Painter, S. 64
Painting 50
 19th century 442
 20th century 442
 history 441−443
Painting, landscape 447
Palmer, R. R. 86, 100, 162
Papacy
 relations with France 166
Papermaking
 18th century 395
Paris 5, 25
 administration 321
 guides 38−39, 41
 siege 1870-71 117
The Paris basin 25
Paris Commune, 1871 116−117
The Paris Commune: an episode in the history of the socialist movement 116
Paris Commune of 1871 116
Paris Herald: the incredible newspaper 487
Paris in the Terror: June, 1793-July, 1794 101
Paris-Match 541
Park, J. 6
Parlements
 18th century 87
Parliament
 19th century 118
 20th century 118, 136
 deputies 329
 election 329
 Fifth Republic 304−305
 Fourth Republic 318−319
 senators 329
 Third Republic 320

Parliament of France 318
Parliament, parties, and society in France, 1946-1958 319
Parliamentary system
 Fourth Republic 263
Parnassian school 424
Pascal, Blaise 170
Pasteur, Louis 398
Paterson, J. 23
Le Patourel, J. 63
Patriotism
 19th century 119
 20th century 119, 121
Patterns of government: the major political systems of Europe 256
Pattison, L. A. 284
Paul, M. K. 201
Paxton, R. O. 130
Pays de Retz
 folklore 159
Peasants
 17th century 75
 18th century 84, 206
 19th century 206
 20th century 202−205, 373
Peasants against politics: rural organizations in Brittany, 1911-1967 205
Péguy, Charles 119
Pemberton, J. E. 540
Periodical articles
 bibliographies 541
Periodicals
 bibliographies 540
 Catholic 506
 cinema 508
 for women 505, 511
 labour movements 364
 monthly 503−504, 506, 511, 514
 on culture 525
 on French language teaching 509, 521, 523
 on history 510, 518, 522
 on literature 519, 524
 on politics 520
 on social sciences 519−520
 television 508
 twice-monthly 517
 weekly 502, 505, 507, 512−513, 515
Perrault, Charles 159
Peterson, A. F. 148−149
Petroleum industries 357
Petroleum supplies
 policy 380

Peyrane, Vaucluse 204
Phenomenology 183
Philippe d'Orléans 84
Phillips, Catherine A. 92
Philosophes, Les 162, 173—174
  18th century 192
Philosophic thought in France and the United States: essays representing trends in contemporary French and American philosophy 183
Philosophy 6, 50, 169
  16th century 71
  18th century 162, 170—177, 192
  19th century 170, 180—181
  20th century 181—183, 190
  bibliographies 181, 540, 542
Phrase books 40
Physical geography 35
Pi-Sunyer, O. 237
Pickles, D. 128, 136, 302
Picon, G. 429
Pierce, R. 195
Piggott, S. 44
Pinchemel, P. 20
Pinder, J. 143
Pinget, Robert 436—438
Pinkney, D. H. 110
Pitts, J. R. 15
Plamenatz, J. P. 108
La Planche, Jean 185
Plantier, Thérèse 431
Pleasure 5, 9
Pleynet, Marcelin 519
Plodemet: report from a French village 209
Pode, M. H. D. 349
Poetry
  19th century 423—425, 427—428
  20th century 425, 427—429
  bibliographies 540
  history 423—425, 427—429
Poets, Women 431
Poitou
  folklore 159
Political geography 35—36
Political parties 273—281
  20th century 256
  Fifth Republic 259
  Fourth Republic 263
Political parties and elections in the French Fifth Republic 259
Political satire
  periodicals 502

Political strategies for industrial order: state, market, and industry in France 355
Political systems
  20th century 256—257
  Fifth Republic 260—262
  Fourth Republic 255
Political theory
  18th century 192
  19th century 196
  20th century 195—196, 198—199, 201—202
  corporatism 193
Politicians
  20th century 257
  Fifth Republic 309
Politics 2—3, 5, 15, 17, 19—20, 255—265, 438
  16th century 66
  17th century 72—73
  19th century 107, 112, 115, 118
  20th century 12, 115, 118, 121, 136, 208—209
  Carolingian 56
  Fifth Republic 302, 304
  history 45, 81, 169
Politics in France 257
Politics of resistance in France, 1940-1944 134
Politics, power, and bureaucracy in France: the administrative élite 314
Politique extérieure de la Cinquième République 284
Pompidou, Georges 286
Ponchie, Jean-P. 541
Ponder, T. C. 379
Pont-de-Monvert: social structure and politics in a French village, 1700-1914 206
Pontalis, J. B. 185
Popular Front 275
Population 20, 24
  19th century 254, 345
  20th century 345
  censuses 252
  migration effects 220, 340
  statistics 250, 253
  women 254
Porcelain 451—452
Portrait, Penelope 360
Portuguese immigrants 236
Post-Impressionism
  history 448

Post-Impressionism: from Van Gogh to Gauguin 448
Postan, C. 65
Poster, M. 200
Poujadist party 266
Poulain, R. 385
Power
 1985 plan 379
 EEC policies 378
Prache, A. 459
Prager, Marie-Françoise 431
Prefectoral Corps 317
Prefects and provincial France 317
Prefectures
 organization 321
Prehistory 42—44
Presidency
 Fifth Republic 306
Press 486
 bibliographies 540
Press, Clandestine
 World War II 133
Price of glory: Verdun, 1916 122
Price, R. 111—112
Prices 341
 statistics 250, 253
Prieur de la Côte d'Or, Claude Antoine 100
Prieur de la Marne, Pierre Louis 100
Prieur-Duvernois, Claude Antoine, comte de 100
Prime Minister
 Fifth Republic 306
Principaux résultats du recensement de 1975 252
Printing
 16th century 68—69
Productivity
 20th century 332, 341
 history 332
Professional associations 352
Promotion and control of industry in postwar France 353
Pronunciation 403
Property law 325
Prophets of Paris 191
Prost, A. 224
Protestantism
 19th century 163
 history 167
Proust, Marcel 418, 422, 430
Prouverelle, E. 530

Psychoanalysis 185—186
Psychoanalytic politics: Freud's French Revolution 186
Psychology
 18th century 176
 history 169
Public administration in France 312
Public affairs 312
Public enterprise 312, 315
Public health 217
Publications statistiques des administrations 251
Publishing 484—485
Pyrenees
 folklore 159

Q

Queneau, Raymond 436, 438
Quotations, Literary 409

R

Rabaud, Henri 471
Racine, Jean 415, 478
Radio reviews 515
Rahv, B. T. 434
Railway industries 376
Railways 397
 history 376
Ramsey, Matthew 399
Rationalism
 17th century 177
 18th century 162, 171—174
Ravel, Maurice 471, 473
Readman, P. 349
Réalités 541
Rebellious century, 1830-1930 109
Recherche sur la pollution atmosphérique: 1972-1975 381
Recht, R. 459
Recipes 383
 bread 389
Recordings, Music 474
Red and the white: report from a French village 209
Redfern, J. 401
Reece, J. E. 240
Reeds, M. 347

169

Regional development 25
Regions 25
 climate 27
 guides 39
 social geography 28
Reign of Terror, 1793-94 100−101
Religion 6, 36, 81, 83
 15th century 62
 16th century 69
 17th century 73, 75
 18th century 162
 19th century 107−108, 163, 180
 20th century 165, 208, 262
 bibliographies 540, 542
 Gallo-Roman 52−53
 history 161−163, 165, 169, 180
Religion and commerce 358
Religious art 165, 439
Religious art in France: the twelfth century 439
Remond, René 266, 518
Renaissance, The 66, 68−71
Renaissance dances 475
The Renaissance in France 68
Renan, Ernest 119, 170
Rendel, M. 308
Répertoire des bibliothèques et organismes de documentation 535
Répertoire des musées de France et de la Communauté 531
Republican movement 78
Resistance movements, 1940-44 131−134
Resources, Natural 20
Restaurants 38
Retirement 214−215
Revolt of the nobles 87
Revolution 1789 78, 86, 88−89, 91−93, 95, 97, 99
 bibliographies 90, 94
 historiography 98
 illustrations 96
 role of the middle classes 103
Revolution 1793-94 179
Revolution 1830 110
Revolution 1848 111−112
Revolution and reaction: 1848 and the Second French Republic 112
Revolutionary movement in France, 1815-1871 108

Revolutionary syndicalism and French labor: a cause without rebels 367
Revolutionary syndicalism in France: the direct action of its time 366
Revolutions
 19th century 108−109
Rewald, J. 446, 448
Ricardou, Jean 437
Richardson, N. J. M. 47
Riché, P. 59
Richelieu, Armand Jean du Plessis, cardinal de 76−77
Richet, D. 88
Rickard, P. 400
Ridley, F. 312
Ridley, F. F. 311, 366
Right wing in France: from 1815 to De Gaulle 266
Right-wing parties 259
 19th century 266−267
 20th century 262, 266−269
Rimbaud, Arthur 425, 427
Rise and fall of New France 151
Rivette, Jacques 483
Riviera
 guides 39
Road maps 34
Road transport 374
Robbe-Grillet, Alain 433−437
Robespierre, Maximilien de 92, 100−101
Rohmer, Eric 483
Roman France 52
Roman Gaul 53
Roman Gaul 43, 52−53
Roman occupation 43, 52−53
Romanticism, Literary 416, 420, 423
 opponents 424
Root, W. 382
Roots of identity, three national movements in contemporary European politics 238
Ropartz, Joseph-Marie-Guy 471
Ross, J. 257
Ross, Jennie-K. 215
Rossiter, S. 41
Rothstein, Marian 70
Roudiez, L. S. 437
Rousseau, Jean Jacques 170
Rousseau, Théodore 447
Roussel, Albert 471
Roussel, Raymond 437
Royalist parties 266, 268−269
Royalty 51
 Merovingian 55

Rubenstein, J. M. 466
Rubin, W. S. 449
Ruffécois
  folklore 159
Rules of the game in Paris 13
Rural development
  20th century 373
Rural life
  18th century 206
  19th century 206
  20th century 203−205, 207−209
Rural revolution in France: the peasantry in the twentieth century 373
Russia and France 83
Russian immigrants 236

S

Saar-Lorraine 25
Sadoul, G. 482
Sadoun, R. 216
Safran, W. 260
Saint André, André Jeanbon 100
Saint-Denis 41
Saint-Evremond, Charles de 175
Saint-Exupéry, Antoine de 194
Saint-Just, Louis de 100
Saint-Laurent, Yves 360
Saint-Simon, Claude Henri, comte de 191
Salacrou, Armand 480
Salager, Annie 431
Salic law 55
Salmon, J. H. M. 66
Salt, J. 220
Saltworks 397
Sand, George 46
Saporta, Marc 437
Saposs, David 363
Sarraute, Nathalie 435−437
Sartre, Jean-Paul 182, 194−195, 200, 276, 434, 480, 520
Satie, Erik 471, 473
Savage, G. 450−451
Savage war of peace: Algeria, 1954-1962 139
Savings schemes 349
Savoy
  folklore 159
Scargill, D. I. 25
Scarth, A. 28
Scheineman, L. 297, 304
Schmidt, C. 533

Schnapp, A. 234
Schoenbrunn, D. 7
Schools 222
  Catholic 164
Schwartz, B. 231, 325−326
Science 6, 50, 398
  18th century 392
  19th century 180−181, 392, 396
  20th century 137, 181
  bibliographies 540
  dictionaries 407
  encyclopaedias 526
  history 169, 390−392, 395−396
  museums 397
  national policy 393−394
  periodicals 515
Scientific societies 391
Scientists and society 396
Scientist's role in society: a comparative study 396
Scott, K. W. 429
Sculpture 50, 450
Second Republic 111−112
Secondary schools 231
Secular religions in France, 1815-1870 180
Senior citizens 214−215
Serant, P. 235
Serfdom 58
Servan-Schreiber, Jean-J. 198
Seventeenth- and eighteenth-century French porcelain 451
Sex 5
Sharp, W. R. 320
Sheahan, J. 353
Sheridan-Smith, A. 209
Shirer, W. L. 123
Short history of France from early times to 1972 47
Short history of French literature 410
Short history of the French Revolution, 1789-1799 99
Shorter, E. 368
Sieberg, Friedrich 11
Siegfried, A. 8
Silva, Milton da 237
Silver, C. B. 213
Silverman, M. 216
Simon, A. L. 387
Simon, Claude 435−437
Simon, J. K. 430
Simon, Michel 262
Siwek-Pouydessau, Jeanne 315
Six, Les 473
Slang 406

171

Slavery 58
Slavery and serfdom in the Middle Ages: selected essays 58
Smith, C. 182
Smith, T. 141
Smock, A. C. 213
Smouts, Marie-C. 300
Soboul, A. 99
Social change 10, 14—15, 19, 24, 81, 83, 191
  15th century 62
  16th century 66
  17th century 72—73, 75
  18th century 84—85, 103, 206
  19th century 107, 113—114, 206
  20th century 114, 136—137, 150, 164, 188, 194, 201—205, 207—209, 211
  Catholic 165
  Fifth Republic 334
  women's role 212—213
Social economy of France 334
Social geography 28
Social history 45
Social institutions 334
Social origins of the French Revolution: the debate on the role of the middle classes 103
Social sciences
  periodicals 515, 519
Social theory
  history 169
Social unrest
  17th century 76
  19th century 109, 111
Social welfare 217
  Third Republic 320
Social welfare in France 217
Socialism
  19th century 365
Socialist party 259, 272
Society and literature 410
Society for French Historical Studies 522
Society for French Studies 524
Society in crisis: France in the sixteenth century 66
Society of Arcueil: a view of French science at the time of Napoleon 391
Society of Friends of the Constitution 102

SOE in France: an account of the British Special Operations Executive in France, 1940-1944 135
Sollers, Philippe 435, 437
Sondheimer, J. 370
Sources de l'histoire de France depuis 1789 aux Archives Nationales 533
Spanish immigrants 236
Spears, Sir Edward 125
Special Operations Executive
  activities in France, 1940-44 135
Spinelli, D. C. 542
Spirit of France 4
Splendid century: some aspects of life in the reign of Louis XIV 75
Spooner, F. C. 343
State and society in France 312
State, Functions of the
  Fourth Republic 335
Statistics 250, 253, 529
  20th century 341
  bibliographies 251
Steam transport
  18th century 395
Stearns, P. N. 214, 367
Steel industries 353
Steel, R. 198
Stein, H. 533
Stendhal, Henri Beyle 418, 421—422
Stewart, J. H. 93
Stiefbold, A. E. 279
Stoianovich, T. 187
Stone, D. 67
Stozier Library, Florida State University 90
Strange defeat 126
The stranger 434
Strikes 366, 368
Strikes in France, 1830-1968 368
Striptease 9
Structuralists 430
Students 233—234
Sturrock, J. 435
Style in the French novel 418
Sudreau Report, 1975 369
Suleiman, E. N. 211, 262, 314, 357
Sun King 74
Sunset of the splendid century 75
Supersonic aircraft industry 375
Supervielle, Jules 427
Suret-Canale, J. 155
Surrealism 430, 449, 479
Sweets, J. 134

Sydenham, M. J. 95, 104
Symbolism, Literary 416, 425
Symcox, G. 99
Syndicalism 366—367
Syndicat National de l'Edition 485
Syntax 402

T

Tables Trimestrielles des Nouveautés 539
Tacit alliance: France and Israel from Suez to the Six-Day War 295
Taine, Hippolyte 98, 119, 170
Tannenbaum, E. R. 14, 269
Tapestry 450, 453
Tapie, V. L. 77
Tarrow, S. 278, 323
Teacher training 231
Technical training 358
Technocracy 311—312
Technocrats
 20th century 262
Technology
 bibliographies 540
 dictionaries 407
 encyclopaedias 526
 history 390, 395
 museums 397
 national policy 393—394
Teilhard de Chardin, Pierre 194
Telegraphy
 18th century 395
Television
 periodicals 508
Television reviews 515
La Tène culture 43
Terminology, literary 401
Terreur, La, 1793-94 100—101
Textbook publishing 484
Textile industries 357
Textiles
 18th century 395
Thabault, R. 113
Theatre 6, 50, 477—480
 bibliographies 540
Theatre in Dada and Surrealism 479
Themes in French culture 16
Third Republic
 history 115, 118, 123, 137
Third World aid 283
Thirty Years' War 77
Thomas, D. H. 532
Thompson, I. B. 21, 24—25

Thomson, D. 196
Thorez, Maurice 277
Thorpe, L. 54
Three faces of fascism 270
Three hundred years of French architecture, 1494-1794 458
Tiersky, R. 274
Tilley, A. 50
Tilly, C. 109, 368
Tilly, L. 109
Tilly, R. 109
Time of glory: the Renaissance in France, 1488-1559 68
Tint, H. 119, 283
Tomorrow's education: the French experience 226
Topography 20—21, 23
Toulouse-Lautrec, Henri de 444
Touring
 maps 34
Tourist guides 38—41
Towards a new democracy 197
Town planning 466—467
Towns
 17th century 73, 75
 18th century 84
Trade
 16th century 343
 17th century 73, 343
 18th century 84
 19th century 345
 20th century 332, 345
 history 332
 statistics 250, 253
Trade unions 336, 352
 19th century 362
 20th century 362
Tragedy
 16th century 477
 17th century 477—478
 history 477—478
Transport 18, 374—375
 statistics 250, 253
Travel
 16th century 68
 architectural tours 455
 bibliographies 540
Travel guides 38—41
Treaties 328
Tregear, P. 113
Tripier, Philippe 140
Trollope, C. 20
Truffaut, François 483
Tuppen, J. N. 374
Turgeon, C. 383

173

Turgot, Anne Robert Jacques, baron de l'Aulne 191
Turkle, S. 186
Twelve who ruled: the year of the Terror in the French Revolution 100

U

Ukiyo-e woodcuts
 influence on French art 444
Ukrainian immigrants 243
Ulam, A. B. 256
Ullmann, S. 418
Ultraroyalist party
 19th century 266
Unemployment 347
Ungaro 360
Union of the Left 280
United States of America
 influence on France 198
Universities 222, 230, 232−234
 20th century 262
Upper classes
 20th century 202
Urban design 466−467
Urban development in Western Europe: France and Belgium 467
Urbanization
 19th century 345
 20th century 345
USA
 impact of French culture 290−291
Utilitarianism
 18th century 192
Utopianism 191

V

Valéry, Paul 425, 427, 430
Van De Walle, E. 254
Vanishing peasant: innovation and change in French agriculture 203
Varèse, Edgard 473
Vennewitz, L. 270
Verdun
 battle, 1916 122
Verlaine, Paul 425, 427
Versailles 41
Via Regia 56

Vichy France: old guard and new order, 1940-1944 130
Vichy government, 1940-44 127−131, 134
 history 150
Vichy regime, 1940-44 129
Vidal-Naquet, P. 234
Vigny, Alfred, comte de 423
Vikings, The 56
Village in the Vaucluse 204
Vincennes 41
Vineyards 385
Viticulture 371, 385
Vizetelly, H. 388
Voltairianism
 19th century 163
Voyages
 17th century 75
Vries, Louis De 407

W

Wages 341
Wahl, N. 331
Wallace-Hadrill, J. M. 55−56, 303
Wallen, C. C. 27
War in France and Flanders, 1939-1940 125
Ward, J. P. 346
Ward, W. H. 463
Warnecke, S. J. 357
Warner, C. K. 371
Weather 27
Weber, E. 121, 268
Week France fell 124
Weightman, J. G. 232
Weile, Simone 195
Welfare services 217, 312
Wellard, J. H. 218
Werth, A. 127
West, T. W. 456
White, R. J. 173
Who are these French? 11
Who's Whos 528
Wilenski, R. H. 441−442
Williams, P. M. 263, 305
Wilson, F. L. 281
Wilson, J. S. G. 351
Windmills 397
Wine 385−386
Wine industry 371
Winegrowers of France and the government since 1875 371
Wines and vineyards of France 385

174

Wines of France 386
Wissous 207
Witchcraft 71
  Jura region 168
Witchcraft in France and Switzerland: the borderlands during the Reformation 168
Wohl, R. 275
Women 5, 212
  17th century 75
  20th century 213
  education 75
  periodicals 505
  poets 431
  statistics 254
  writers 412
Women and the law 325
Women in Europe since 1750 212
Women: roles and status in eight countries 213
Women writers in France: variations on a theme 412
Woodward, D. 338
Worker-priests 165
Working classes
  Fourth Republic 264
Working conditions 217
World of fashion: people, places, resources 361
World of the office worker 210
World War I
  Verdun, 1916 122
World War II 83
  France, 1939-40 123
  France, 1940 124–126
  French clandestine press 133
  French resistance movements 131–134
  occupation of France 127–131, 133
  SOE activities in France 135
Worth, Charles Frederick 360
Woshinsky, O. H. 309
Wrestling 9
Wright, G. 78, 373
Wright, Vincent 262
Writers, Women 412
Wrong, G. M. 151
Wylie, L. 15, 204, 208
Wyon, O. 1

Y

Your guide to French pronunciation 403
Yugoslav immigrants 236

Z

Zeldin, T. 107, 114, 230
Zola, Emile 422
Zysman, J. 355

Map of France

This map shows the more important towns and other features.

Z
2161
C5
1980